Good

Alby Hailes

Vibes

Good

Alby
Hailes

Eat well with
feel-good
flavours

Vibes

HarperCollins*Publishers*

HarperCollins_Publishers_

Australia • Brazil • Canada • France • Germany • Holland • India
Italy • Japan • Mexico • New Zealand • Poland • Spain • Sweden
Switzerland • United Kingdom • United States of America

First published in 2023
by HarperCollinsPublishers (New Zealand) Limited
Unit D1, 63 Apollo Drive, Rosedale, Auckland 0632, New Zealand
harpercollins.co.nz

A catalogue record for this book is available from the National Library of New Zealand

ISBN 978 1 775 542 247

Cover and internal design by George Saad
Publisher: Holly Hunter
Project editor: Rachel Cramp
Recipe editor: Tracy Rutherford
Index by Rachel Cramp and Belinda Yuille
Colour reproduction by Splitting Image Colour Studio, Wantirna, Victoria
Printed and bound in China by 1010 Printing

8 7 6 5 4 3 2 1   23 24 25 26

Introduction

Good Vibes is a celebration of food and flavours that make us feel good.

These are joyful, inventive and colourful recipes designed to ignite a love of food and bring people together. Nothing in this book is vanilla – other than the odd splash of vanilla extract. Inside you'll find recipes to inspire the palate and brighten the table, to nourish, dazzle and warm the heart.

Rediscovering the joy of food can mean going back to basics and trying to connect on a personal level, beyond the contradictory messages of what you should or shouldn't eat. Ask yourself: How does this meal make me feel? Do I know the ingredients I am eating? How am I connecting to the smells, texture and taste? What does good food look like for me?

Having worked as a doctor in mental health, I know just how fundamentally our food choices influence our attitudes and emotions. If we have fun with flavours, try new things and eat mindfully, food takes on greater meaning than its caloric intake.

A joyful approach to food is not just about the eating, but about the making and sharing. Cooking is a time to unwind: the careful chopping of garlic, the grinding of spices, the bubble of simmering rice, with your favourite music and a boogie in the kitchen. Giving time and attention to the food we eat, and finding enjoyment within it, is like giving ourselves an edible hug. The sharing of food takes this further; a simple act of love and service for others can be a powerful thing.

While the flavours in this book are designed to nourish your mental health, the ingredients are also nutritionally balanced to benefit your physical health. Focused around seasonal wholefoods, of the almost 120 recipes in these pages, you'll find over 50% are vegan and at least 80% are vegetarian. I hope that meat-eaters will lean in to reducing their consumption, but this food should be accessible to everyone. The recipes speak to balance and the importance of food in bringing us together. On each recipe you'll find a symbol to help you eat seasonally and within your dietary focus.

(VE) Vegan

(VEᵒ) Vegan option

(GF) Gluten-free

(S) Spring

(S) Summer

(A) Autumn

(W) Winter

Each chapter of this book focuses on the feeling and intention that your food should bring; these are the good vibes to channel as you cook.

Energise is about kickstarting your day in style, with breakfast and brunch food to jump out of bed for; like the Turkish-inspired Breakfast gözleme with preserved lemon mayo (page 38) or effortlessly delicious Cilbir eggs with curry leaves & saffron yoghurt (page 28).

Connect is the largest chapter, filled with recipes to place in the centre of the table for hungry hands and spoons to dig in and devour. Many are layered sharing plates that can be paired with a main or become part of a larger spread, such as Citrus-roasted broccolini with hazelnut romesco, rocket & mint (page 81). Some are salads, perfect for barbecue parties – the Grilled sweetcorn & nectarine salad with miso dressing (page 82) is a favourite – or winter potlucks. Others are tarts and breads to slice and share, like Persimmon & red onion tarte Tatin with crispy sage & feta (page 42), or recipes that encourage your guests to join you in the kitchen for assembly: think dumplings, tacos, samosas and bao.

Thrive is all about big flavour and minimal effort; speedy meals designed for weeknight cooking. We're talking soups, curries, dals and pastas, food to pile into bowls and chow down on. Many of these are played on repeat in my home, like 'The OG' mango & mandarin curry (page 108) or Drunken meatballs (page 123). Nourishing food that's stress-free to cook.

Comfort is filled with warming soul food, like hearty bowls of Beetroot & jackfruit chilli with sour yoghurt (page 150) or the deeply satisfying Stuffed aubergines with crimson sauce & green caper oil (page 140). Some of these recipes are about taking it slow, such as melt-in-the-mouth Coffee & cardamom braised beef cheeks (page 163) or creamy Herb, onion & hazelnut cheesecake with blistered tomatoes (page 154). You'll also find fresh takes on classic comfort foods we all know and love.

Delight is your happy place, full of inspired desserts, cakes and bakes that surprise and satisfy. These are creamy, crunchy, boozy, fruity and daringly delicious, like the Chilli, chocolate & orange 'impossible' cake (page 206) or Fig baklava nests with orange blossom syrup (page 199). Because sweetness in life is essential.

Sustain is just that: a collection of staples that feature throughout, either forming the base of other hero recipes, or to have on hand in your pantry or fridge for serving on the side.

I've spent years cooking, developing, writing and re-writing recipes to share here with you in this, my first cookbook. I've published multiple food blogs under different names. I've even put myself out there – and won! – on a reality TV cooking show, and now I'm ready to share the food I love most with home cooks of New Zealand and the world. My name is Alby Hailes, welcome to my kitchen.

ALBY HAILES

How to: flavour

Flavour has always been at the forefront of my life in the kitchen. Fans of food writers Nik Sharma, Yotam Ottolenghi and Anna Jones will notice their globally inspired influence on my recipes. I learned about new ingredients and textures from cooks such as these, and then used those ideas as a base for my own experimentation. In the same way, the recipes in my book aim to inspire, to act as a canvas for anyone to develop intuition and style in the kitchen.

The beauty of food is seeing how otherwise distant and distinct flavours and textures can form something uniquely delicious. For me, this beauty can be broken down into six critical elements: *Sour/Acid* (e.g. citrus, vinegar, tamarind); *Sweet* (e.g. sugar, fruits, maple syrup); *Fat* (e.g. butter, oil, avocado); *Umami/ Savoury* (e.g. mushrooms, tomatoes, meat); *Salinity* (e.g. salt, feta, olives) and *Heat* (e.g. chilli, ginger, black pepper).

Like edible chemistry, these are the factors I attempt to balance in everything that I cook. Roasted aubergines with cherry toms, tamarind sauce & sesame labneh (page 65) combines a creamy yoghurt base of fat and acid, umami aubergines and tomatoes, and a tamarind sauce that brings the sweet, sour, salt and chilli heat. Black sesame, rose & cardamom cake with honey mascarpone icing (page 179) combines butter, salt and oil, black pepper for heat, honey sweetness, black sesame umami, and a hint of sour from the mascarpone icing.

These recipes will encourage you to be fearless with flavour and get excited about the unexpected. There is nothing more thrilling than developing your own taste in the kitchen, making food work for you.

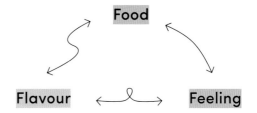

Food not only fuels our bodies, it impacts our mood. Only recently has science started looking at this link between mood and food, and the strongest evidence points towards diets focused on a balanced wholefoods approach that minimises processed and packaged goods. While certain foods boost your mood at a cellular level, such as foods high in omega-3 fatty acids, the mood–food relationship is usually more personal: nostalgia from familiar favourites, visual appeal or the excitement of trying something new. Often it is flavour that has the greatest effect, like the satisfying sweetness of a ripe nectarine or the calming quality of cucumber.

Just as food and flavour can create a feeling, the reverse is also true – our food choices are often dependent on our mood. When we're stressed, we will look for convenience; when we're motivated, we might cook something new. Similarly, how we feel influences how food tastes. If you're tired or angry, then the food you eat is often less appetising; and in my experience, things always taste better when you're relaxing on holiday. Food, flavour and feeling are inseparable.

Use this map as a reference, not a rule, to help understand what's behind your favourite flavours. This is what positive eating is all about.

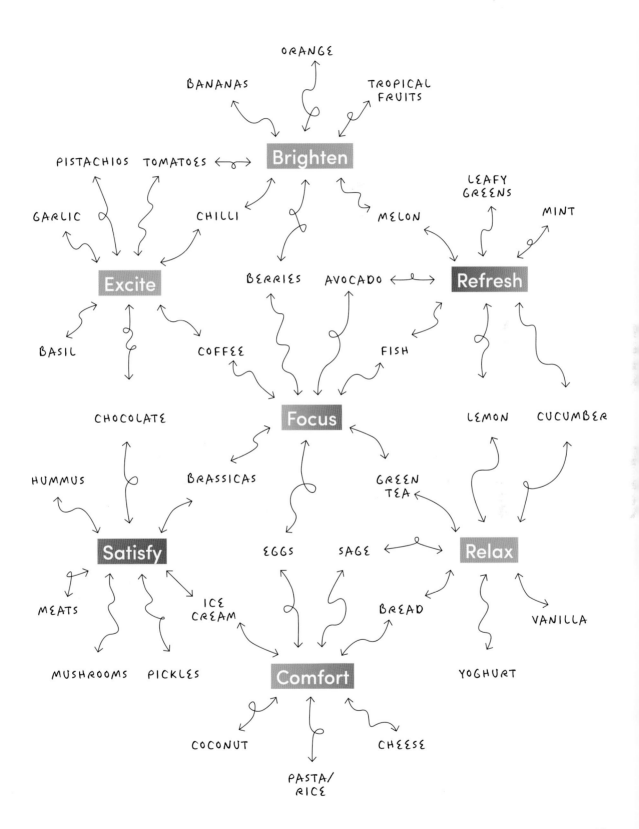

A little bit different: flavour glossary

Most of the recipes in this book have strong foundations in pantry basics and common spices that have become mainstream staples in home kitchens. However, there are ingredients that may be a little less familiar. Fortunately, global flavours are now at our fingertips, and all these ingredients can be found at most supermarkets and international food stores. Many have now become essentials in my culinary toolbox.

Spices, seeds & stalks

Amchur: This spice powder is made from sun-dried strips of unripe green mangoes, with a relatively coarse texture and tropical aroma. Its bittersweet sourness goes well in curries and soups.

Black tahini: This paste made from ground black sesame seeds is often used in Asian cooking, offering a bold grey-black pigment to food. The flavour is similarly nutty but slightly more bitter than regular tahini.

Cardamom: One of my favourite spices, cardamom gives a complex herbal warmth with subtle sweetness. I prefer to use green cardamom, commonly known as 'true cardamom', as its flavour is heftier – the whole pods can be thrown into curries, or the seeds crushed to a powder for use in sweet and savoury dishes.

Curry leaves: Picked from the curry tree, *Murraya koenigii*, these tangy, slightly bitter leaves are commonly used to form the base of Indian and Sri Lankan curries. They are sold fresh or dried and can be easily sourced from most Indian food stores. I recommend purchasing a plant from your local nursery – they are low maintenance, and the leaves can be sporadically picked and frozen for year-round use. I like to fry the fresh leaves in hot oil to use them as an aromatic crispy garnish.

Fennel seeds: These sweet, aniseed-tasting seeds have long been used in both Italian cooking and certain regions of India to flavour meats, sweets, breads or curries, either in their whole form or dry-toasted then ground. The fragrance of this spice would have to be one of my favourites.

Kaffir lime leaves: Also called makrut lime, these unusual hourglass-shaped leaves bring a distinctly citrus scent and flavour to dishes. The fresh leaves are typically used in South-East Asian cuisine and can also be grown well in some New Zealand climates.

Kawakawa leaves: The kawakawa plant, *Piper excelsum*, has long been used in rongoā Māori for its anti-inflammatory effect, among other healing properties. The flowers are also edible, but I like the leaves for the peppery bitterness they impart. You can use the fresh leaves to infuse sauces and broths, or grind the dry leaves to a powder. The leaves can also be fried in oil for a crunchy and decorative effect.

Lemongrass: This large green grass, *Cymbopogon citratus*, is native to Southeast Asia. The stems are used to give a soft lemon flavour and gorgeous aroma, perfect for teas, curries and dipping sauces.

Matcha: A powder made from finely ground leaves of the green tea plant *Camellia sinensis*. These are shade-grown before harvest to increase theanine levels, an amino acid that gives matcha its distinct umami flavour.

It is often used in traditional Japanese tea ceremonies, and I like to use it in baking for its mellow grassiness and soft green pigment.

Saffron: Renowned as the most expensive spice in the world by weight, fortunately a little goes a long way. The dried vibrant orange-red stigma of *Crocus sativus* flowers impart a remarkable golden colour to food. Its flavour is complex, simultaneously floral and honey-like, while also grounded in a certain earthiness. Saffron's magic is brought out best by steeping the strands in a warm liquid before adding to sweet or savoury dishes.

Star anise: The seeds and seed pod from *Illicium verum*, an evergreen tree native to China, can be used in its whole star form to infuse soups and curries, or ground to a powder for use in rubs, marinades or baked goods. It has a slightly sweet aniseed flavour, reminiscent of liquorice, and goes excellently with citrus, meats and vanilla.

Sumac: A ferrous-red powder ground from the dried sour berries of the Middle Eastern shrub, *Rhus coriaria*. It has a subtle fruity sourness, which pairs well with onions, grilled meats and fish, offering a welcome tartness.

Tahini: Made from ground sesame seeds, this oily paste is a ubiquitous condiment in Middle Eastern cooking, most widely known for its place in traditional hummus. I find that it lends itself equally well to sweet and savoury cooking, with its addictive nutty flavour and smooth texture.

Ferments, florals & fruits

Ancho chillies: The dried version of Mexican poblano chillies, sold either whole or ground, these chillies bring a slightly sweet and smoky flavour and mild heat to sauces and marinades. They are found at most specialty food stores.

Capers: The flower buds of the caper bush, *Capparis spinosa*, are salted and pickled to create a flavour powerhouse that smacks of citrus tang, brininess and floral quality. They make an excellent base for dressings or can be fried until crunchy as a sprinkled flavour bomb.

Gochujang: A fermented red chilli paste used in Korean cooking, with a slightly sweet, spicy and deep umami flavour. It is well-known globally for its use in the traditional Korean rice dish bibimbap, and I like to use it as a base for warming soups, stews and noodle dishes.

Mirin: This sweet and slightly syrupy fermented rice wine brings brightness, sweetness and subtle umami when added to savoury dishes.

Miso: The ultimate in umami, this Japanese paste made from fermented soy beans gives you all the sweet, salty and savoury feels. Shiro (white) miso paste is a favourite of mine to add punch to salad dressings or flavour interest in sweet dishes.

Orange blossom water: Prepared similarly to the more ubiquitous rose water, this is made using the blossoms of the bitter Seville orange. It gives a perfumed citrus aroma and flavour that I love to use in baking and as the base of syrups when roasting or poaching fruits.

Pomegranate molasses: This syrup, traditionally used in Middle Eastern cooking, is made through the evaporation of fresh pomegranate juice to form a sweet and tangy concentrate. You'll find I use this frequently in dressings and sauces, as it brings a sharp, slightly acid sweetness that can provide an instant flavour lift.

Preserved lemons: Preserved lemons are commonly used in North African and Indian cooking, in soups, stews and sauces, to bring serious citrus punch. Fresh lemons are packed with salt, jarred, and left to ferment, which sees the skin develop an intense lemon flavour with slightly funky, salty undertones. It also allows you to use the whole lemon – in fact it is the skin of preserved lemons that I like to use in my cooking rather than the flesh, to give a citrus-umami hit. I recommend preserving your own lemons (page 218) as it's so easy to do, or they can be found at specialty food stores and some supermarkets.

Rose harissa: With its origins in North African cuisine, this chilli paste is traditionally made with roasted red peppers, spices, herbs and rose petals and/or rose water. Its heat can vary in store-bought varieties, so always taste and test. I encourage you to make the version in the Sustain chapter, which smacks of rose, lemon, garlic and aniseed. It's the perfect base for spicy curries, soups and marinades.

Rose water: Steeping rose petals in water allows the essential oils to infuse into the liquid, creating a perfectly perfumed water that adds a distinctive floral flavour. I like to use this both in baking and when making Moroccan or Indian-inspired eats. The flavour can be polarising (some might find it a bit too floral), so start small – you can always add more.

Tamarind paste: A sweet, tangy paste made from the pulp of the brown podded fruit of the tamarind tree, *Tamarindus indica*. It is used in a wide range of culinary cultures, bringing a sweet and sour flavour to savoury dishes or as the base of chutneys and sweet drinks.

Verjuice: This is the highly acidic juice pressed from unripe grapes. It gives brilliant sourness and acidity with a hint of sweetness to dressings and sauces, without the sometimes overpowering alcoholic component of its fermented cousin, white wine.

A memo on measurements, equipment and ingredients

If there is one thing to go and purchase for your kitchen right now (if you haven't already), it's a basic digital kitchen scale. You can pick one of these up for as little as $10 NZD, and it will be worth its weight in kitchen gold. Cup measurements can be variable, so to ensure consistently accurate outcomes, you will find grams and millilitres used in these recipes.

When it comes to tablespoons and teaspoons, I tend to use ordinary cutlery rather than measuring spoons, so precision is not essential, but for the purposes of clarity: **1 tbsp = 15ml** and **1 tsp = 5ml**.

There are a few other pieces of kitchen equipment that I highly recommend having in your cooking artillery:

- Mortar and pestle – often recipes call for you to toast spices or seeds and then grind them.

- Dutch oven (24–26cm) – perfect for when a recipe begins on the stovetop then bakes in the oven.

- Stick blender (also known as a hand blender or immersion blender) – minimal clean-up required.

- Food processor – some recipes call for things to be blitzed and not puréed (which is what tends to happen if you use a blender).

- Electric hand or stand mixer.

- Kitchen blowtorch – one of my favourite tools to use at home, but it is not essential.

- Digital instant read thermometer – useful for deep-frying, tempering chocolate, etc.

Where possible, cooking seasonally with local ingredients is always recommended.

Butter can be whatever is on hand, salted or unsalted – all recipes work equally well with either. **Eggs** should always be free-range and either size 6 or 7 (medium–large). Unless specified as dried, all **herbs** and leaves are fresh. Try to use **ground spices** that were purchased within 12 months, as their powers will deteriorate beyond this. **Chillies** have their stalks removed and are always used with their seeds included – but you can adjust this based on your own heat preference. **Dark chocolate** is 70% cocoa solids and vegan. **Vanilla extract** is real. **Maple syrup** is 100% pure. **Yoghurt** is always unsweetened, natural and full fat. **Coconut cream** is full fat. **Sea salt** is fine unless otherwise specified, **black pepper** is always freshly cracked.

***

All recipes have been tested using the fan-forced oven function, but conventional temperatures have also been included. Because all ovens run differently, I've tried to describe the appearance you're aiming for as well as the approximate oven time in most recipes, so keep an eye on things and if in doubt, trust your instincts.

Energise

Breakfast boosters

I was in my final year of high school when I stopped eating breakfast. I took music as a subject, which meant that every morning I had a 15-minute cycle from my boarding hostel to another school for 7am lessons. Unfortunately, this early start also meant that I now missed the hostel breakfasts. I didn't realise it, but the 16-year-old me who asked 'Who even needs to eat breakfast anyway?' was robbing himself of energy to get through each day.

So began a five-year period of skipping breakfast, sometimes skipping lunch, and forcing my body to somehow work on water and desperation for much of the day. What started as a small inconvenience was maintained by honest laziness and became a serious case of breakfast neglect. Years later, forced by a change in routine and some deep introspection, I slowly started eating breakfast again. Nowadays, I simply cannot function without it. It's more from a mental than physical perspective – sitting down with a bowl of homemade granola kickstarts my brain and sets my mojo in motion as I tell myself, 'I will own this day.'

Energise is what breakfast should be all about. Firstly, you need something that will give you the energy to be your best self, in both body and mind, for the day ahead. It should also be food you can get excited about – creative, wholesome goodness that begins your day with a bang. This doesn't mean it has to be time-consuming – although try to give yourself an extra few minutes in the morning for some mindful eating. Look to Cilbir eggs with curry leaves & saffron yoghurt (page 28) or Toasted coconut & chocolate porridge with balsamic cherries (page 34) for breakfast ideas that are short on time but major on flavour.

Another way to improve your morning routine is with a little pre-emptive planning. Recipes like my Cashew, fennel & apricot granola (page 24) or A-little-luxe overnight bircher (page 20) can be made in advance. Convenience doesn't have to rely on store-bought cereals and granolas, many of which are packed full of hidden sugars and additives. A little extra effort preparing your own breakfast means that you control what you're putting into your body.

Breakfast shouldn't always be about efficiency. There are times when the morning meal should be treasured, whether it's pancake Sundays with the whānau, breakfast in bed, or a slow brunch with one too many mimosas. It's these moments where last night's dreams are discussed in far too much detail, laughs are shared and plans for the day are pondered.

Rockmelon with pink pom yoghurt & herb sugar

hands-on time	15 mins
total time	15 mins
serves	4–6

(VE) (GF)   S A

My grandmother in her wisdom always told me to eat more fruit for breakfast. This is my answer to her. Ripe melon, bright herbs, thick yoghurt, zingy pomegranate and lime. Simple and fresh, the perfect way to start the day.

First make the herb sugar. Use a mortar and pestle to pound the mint, basil and caster sugar in a circular motion for a minute, until the herbs disintegrate and combine with the sugar. Set aside.

To deseed the pomegranate, cut it in half then hold one half, flesh side down, over a large bowl. Use a wooden spoon to whack the outer skin of the pomegranate to release the seeds into the bowl. Use your fingers to release any remaining pomegranate seeds stuck inside. Repeat with the other half. Remove any white membrane that has fallen into the bowl and discard the skins. You should be left with a hefty amount of seeds sitting in a small amount of juice. Strain the pomegranate juice into a separate bowl.

To make the pink pom yoghurt, take another bowl and whisk the yoghurt until smooth. Add 3 tbsp of the pomegranate juice, 3 tbsp of pomegranate seeds and the orange blossom water. Fold through until just combined.

Cut the rockmelon into quarters and remove the skin, then scoop out the seeds. Slice quarters into 5mm-thick wedges and add to the bowl with the remaining pomegranate seeds. Add the lime juice and toss to coat.

To serve, spoon the yoghurt over a serving platter, smoothing with the back of a spoon to create an even layer. Arrange the melon slices on top and spoon over the remaining pomegranate seeds. Drizzle with any remaining pomegranate juice and dot the herb sugar evenly over the fruit.

Ingredients

- 20 mint leaves
- 10 basil leaves
- 3 tbsp caster sugar
- 1 pomegranate
- 280g yoghurt (coconut or unsweetened natural Greek)
- 1 tbsp orange blossom water
- ½ large or 1 small rockmelon
- freshly squeezed juice of ½ lime

A-little-luxe overnight bircher

hands-on time	10 mins
total time	10 mins (+ overnight soaking)
serves	2

(VE)

This is the ultimate make-ahead breakfast. The brightness of the beetroot bircher and the warming gingerbread and fig bircher are two of my favourite flavour combinations. Prepare for the week by quadrupling the make-ahead ingredients (roasted rhubarb, chopped nuts) so you're ready to mix-and-go each morning. The basic bircher is versatile – use it as a base for whatever flavours you have on hand, such as dried fruits, different spices, berries or grated apple.

Combine the basic bircher ingredients in a medium–large bowl or container, then choose one of the following.

For the beetroot, raspberry, rhubarb & hazelnut bircher, stir in the raspberries, beetroot, maple syrup, vanilla, cinnamon and star anise until well combined. Cover and refrigerate overnight.

The following morning, stir the bircher and divide evenly between two bowls. Serve topped with yoghurt, roasted rhubarb and hazelnuts.

For the gingerbread, fig & pecan bircher, stir in the dried figs, golden syrup, vanilla and spices until well combined. Cover and refrigerate overnight.

The following morning, stir the bircher and divide evenly between two bowls. Serve topped with yoghurt, figs and pecans.

Basic bircher

100g traditional wholegrain rolled oats

2 tbsp chia seeds

finely grated zest of ½ orange

250ml milk (oat or almond)

60ml freshly squeezed orange juice

Beetroot, raspberry, rhubarb & hazelnut bircher

75g fresh or frozen raspberries

½ small beetroot, peeled and finely grated (about 70g)

1 tbsp maple syrup

1 tsp vanilla extract

½ tsp ground cinnamon

¼ tsp ground star anise

yoghurt (coconut or unsweetened natural), to serve

Rose & orange roasted rhubarb (page 222), to serve

50g roasted hazelnuts, roughly chopped, to serve

Gingerbread, fig & pecan bircher

75g dried figs, roughly chopped

1 tbsp golden syrup

2 tsp vanilla extract

½ tsp ground ginger

½ tsp ground cinnamon

¼ tsp mixed spice

pinch of ground nutmeg

yoghurt (coconut or unsweetened natural), to serve

2 fresh figs, quartered, to serve

50g roasted pecans, roughly chopped, to serve

hands-on time	40 mins
total time	1 hour
serves	2–3

Zucchini fritters with avocado feta whip & herb salad

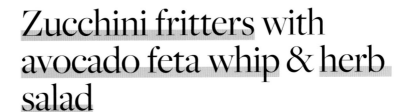

Zucchini fritters

400g zucchini (about 3–4)

½ tsp sea salt

1 tsp fennel seeds

1 tsp cumin seeds

1 tsp black mustard seeds

2 eggs, separated

50g plain flour

1 tsp baking powder

½ tsp cracked black pepper

finely grated zest of 1 lemon

2 tbsp canola oil

Avocado feta whip

100g feta cheese

flesh of 1 small avocado

4 tbsp unsweetened natural yoghurt

¼ tsp ground chilli

squeeze of lemon juice

Herb salad

1 handful fennel fronds or fresh dill

1 handful coriander leaves

1 handful mint leaves

freshly squeezed lemon juice, to serve

This is my weekend breakfast to manage the glut of green goodness in my zucchini patch. Beating the egg whites before folding into the batter is the key to a light, fluffy fritter. And salting and squeezing the grated zucchini ensures the fritters won't be gluggy.

First make the batter for the zucchini fritters. Grate the zucchini and place in a sieve or colander resting over a large bowl. Sprinkle the salt over the zucchini and toss to combine. Leave for 30 minutes, then place the zucchini in a muslin cloth and squeeze out as much liquid as possible. Alternatively, you could squeeze handfuls of the zucchini. Discard the liquid and transfer the zucchini to a large bowl. Set aside.

Toast the fennel, cumin and black mustard seeds in a frying pan over medium-high heat for 2 minutes until fragrant and starting to pop. Use a mortar and pestle to grind to a powder, as finely as you can be bothered. Add the spices to the zucchini. In another bowl, use an electric mixer to beat the egg whites until stiff peaks form. Add half the beaten egg whites, the egg yolks, flour, baking powder, pepper and lemon zest to the zucchini and stir to form a dense batter. Gently fold the remaining beaten egg whites into the batter until just combined. Leave to rest for 5 minutes.

Prepare the avocado feta whip. Crumble the feta into a bowl and add the avocado flesh. Using a fork, mash the feta and avocado together until as smooth as possible. Add the yoghurt and ground chilli and using the fork, mix for a few seconds until nicely whipped. Add a squeeze of lemon juice, then taste and add a little more juice if you like.

To cook the fritters, heat the oil in a frying pan over medium heat. Drop heaped tablespoons of the batter into the oil (you will have to cook the fritters in two batches). Cook for 3–4 minutes, until bubbles start to pop on the surface. Turn over and cook for a further 3–4 minutes, until golden brown and cooked through. Transfer to a paper towel-lined plate and cover with a clean tea towel to keep warm. Repeat with the remaining batter.

For the herb salad, place the herbs in a bowl and toss together.

Serve the fritters warm, with a few dollops of avocado feta whip, a handful of herb salad, and a generous squeeze of lemon juice.

Cashew, fennel & apricot granola

hands-on time	10 mins
total time	45 mins
makes	750g (6–8 servings)

(VE)   S S A W

This breakfast is on repeat in my kitchen. The beauty of granola is that it lends itself to endless variation, and this blend of aromatic fennel, cardamom, sharp apricots and crunchy cashews is a winning combination.

Preheat the oven to 150°C fan-forced (or 170°C conventional). Line 2 large, rimmed oven trays with baking paper.

Use a mortar and pestle to lightly crush the cardamom pods to extract the seeds. Discard the pods, grind the seeds to a rough powder, then transfer to a large bowl. Add the oats, cashews, quinoa, buckwheat, pumpkin seeds, fennel seeds and salt. Stir with a wooden spoon to mix through. In a small bowl, whisk together the olive oil, apple cider vinegar and 85ml of the maple syrup. Pour the liquid over the oat mixture and fold through until evenly coated. Spread evenly onto the two prepared oven trays in a single layer and leave to sit for 10 minutes.

Bake for 30–35 minutes, stirring and swapping the trays after 15 minutes, until golden brown and toasted evenly (cooking time depends on your oven – watch the granola closely). Turn off the oven. Tip the granola back into the mixing bowl and stir through the apricots and remaining maple syrup. Return to the trays and place in the turned off oven. Leave for 1 hour to dry out as the oven cools down. When cooled completely, store in an airtight container.

Serve topped with unsweetened natural yoghurt (coconut or dairy) and your favourite milk.

Note: You can tailor the granola mix, using your favourite ingredients or things you already have on hand. Try any of the following:

- Seeds & such – sunflower seeds, chia seeds, sesame seeds, bran flakes, coconut chips or threads.

- Nuts – hazelnuts, pistachios, peanuts, Brazil nuts, macadamias.

- Spices – cinnamon, cocoa, ginger, cardamom, black pepper.

- Essence – orange blossom water, rose water, vanilla extract.

- Sweetness – honey, brown rice syrup.

- Dried fruits (stir through after baking) – chopped dried figs, sultanas, chopped dates, goji berries.

20 green cardamom pods
200g traditional wholegrain rolled oats
150g cashews
100g quinoa
100g buckwheat groats
75g pumpkin seeds
¾ tsp fennel seeds
½ tsp sea salt
60ml olive oil
1 tbsp apple cider vinegar
115ml maple syrup
100g dried apricots, chopped

(S) (S) (A) (W)

Herb ricotta pancakes with charred greens & chilli-lime syrup

Herb ricotta pancakes

310ml milk

finely grated zest and freshly squeezed juice of 1 lime

50g butter, plus extra for cooking

2 spring onions, finely chopped

3 cloves garlic, finely chopped

3 eggs, separated

250g ricotta

300g plain flour

1 ½ tbsp baking powder

1 tsp ground cumin

½ tsp sea salt

½ tsp cracked black pepper

2 tbsp chopped parsley

2 tbsp chopped mint

2 tbsp chopped coriander

Chilli-lime syrup

6 green cardamom pods

1 tsp fennel seeds

1 tbsp finely grated fresh ginger

½ long green chilli, finely chopped

1 tbsp honey

80g caster sugar

finely grated zest of 3 limes

80ml freshly squeezed lime juice

¼ tsp sea salt

50ml maple syrup

These savoury pancakes are a game-changer. Folding in the beaten whites at the last minute gives a fluffy pancake, and resting the batter ensures the acid and baking powder react for extra height. You should make these for the chilli-lime syrup alone – it's next-level good.

First make the pancake batter. In a large bowl, whisk together the milk, lime zest and juice. Leave for 10 minutes to curdle slightly. In a frying pan over medium heat, stir the butter, spring onion and garlic until the butter has melted and the garlic is starting to turn golden. Transfer to a separate bowl and leave to cool for a minute or two. Add the egg yolks and ricotta and whisk until smooth. Add the egg mixture to the curdled milk and whisk until well combined. In a separate bowl, sift together the flour, baking powder, cumin, salt and pepper. Add the dry ingredients to the wet and whisk until just combined, to form a relatively thick batter. Stir the herbs through. In a separate bowl, use an electric mixer to beat the egg whites until stiff peaks form. Gently fold half the egg whites into the batter, then fold in the rest until just mixed through. Leave to rest for 15 minutes.

Meanwhile, prepare the chilli-lime syrup. Use a mortar and pestle to lightly crush the cardamom pods to open them. Transfer the pods and seeds to a small saucepan. Add the remaining ingredients (except the maple syrup) and 125ml water. Bring to the boil over medium-high heat then reduce the heat slightly to a rapid simmer. Cook, uncovered, for about 7 minutes or until reduced by half and starting to thicken a little to a maple syrup-like consistency. It will thicken further as it cools. Strain through a sieve into a jug, stir in the maple syrup, and set aside to cool.

Preheat the oven to 80°C fan-forced (or 100°C conventional).

To cook the pancakes, melt a knob of butter in a large cast iron or non-stick frying pan over medium heat, tilting the pan to allow the butter to evenly coat the base. Once hot, drop ladles of batter into the pan one or two at a time, depending on desired size. Cook for about 3 minutes, until the surface of the pancake has some bubbles that are just starting to pop. Flip over and cook for a further 3 minutes, until golden brown and cooked through. Repeat with the remaining batter (you do not need to re-butter the pan), adjusting the temperature as you go to achieve a beautiful golden-brown colour. Place the pancakes on a plate in the preheated oven to keep warm while you cook the rest.

Charred greens

2 tbsp canola oil

100g kale, stalks removed, leaves shredded

4 cloves garlic, finely chopped

freshly squeezed juice of ½ lime

¼ tsp sea salt

½ head broccoli, stalk removed, cut into small florets

To serve

70g almonds, roughly chopped

150g mascarpone

chopped fresh herbs (parsley, mint, coriander)

Meanwhile, cook the charred greens. Heat 1 tbsp canola oil in a medium-large frying pan over medium-high heat. Add the kale and garlic and cook for 2 minutes, then add the lime juice, salt and 125ml water. Cook for a further 6 minutes, until the kale is wilted and the water has evaporated. Transfer the kale to a bowl and set aside. Heat the remaining oil in the pan over medium-high heat. Add the broccoli florets and cook for 3 minutes, until slightly charred and cooked but retaining a little crunch. Return the wilted kale to the pan and stir to heat through. Remove from the heat.

To serve, toast the almonds in a frying pan over medium heat for 2–3 minutes, until lightly browned. Place the mascarpone in a small bowl and whip with a fork until smooth. Serve the pancakes warm, topped with the charred greens, a dollop of mascarpone, toasted almonds, chopped fresh herbs and a generous drizzle of chilli-lime syrup.

Cilbir eggs with curry leaves & saffron yoghurt

hands-on time	30 mins
total time	30 mins
serves	2, but easily doubled

GF

The combination of creamy yoghurt, spiced butter and runny yolks is simple yet oh-so satisfying. Known as the breakfast of sultans, in my interpretation of cilbir eggs (or Turkish eggs), saffron is the star of the show and curry leaves give added texture.

First make the saffron yoghurt. Combine the saffron threads and 1 tbsp hot water in a medium bowl and leave for 15 minutes to infuse. Add the yoghurt, garlic, lemon juice and salt. Stir together, pressing the saffron threads with the back of the spoon against the side of the bowl to extract as much of the beautiful yellow saffron pigment as possible. Set aside at room temperature.

To poach the eggs, set a medium–large saucepan with 7cm of water over high heat. Bring to the boil, add the vinegar and reduce the heat so the water is at a gentle simmer, barely bubbling. Line a plate with paper towel and place next to the stovetop. Place a fine mesh sieve over a bowl. Crack one egg into the sieve, shake a little to strain away any watery part of the white and then gently tip the egg into a small ramekin. Repeat with a second egg, transferring gently into a second ramekin. Carefully slide the eggs from the ramekins into the gently simmering water, one on each side of the pan. Poach the eggs for 3 minutes so that the whites are set and the yolks are still runny. Transfer with a slotted spoon to the paper-lined plate to drain. Repeat with the remaining two eggs.

While the final eggs are cooking, melt the butter in a small frying pan over medium heat. Once starting to foam and lightly brown, add the curry leaves and cook for a minute until crispy. Remove from the heat and stir through the olive oil, paprika, chilli flakes and turmeric.

To serve, spoon the saffron yoghurt into the base of two wide shallow bowls. Sit two poached eggs into each bowl of yoghurt. Stir the maple syrup into the spiced butter mixture and pour around and over the eggs, ensuring the crispy curry leaves are shared evenly. Sprinkle with chopped mint and serve immediately with toasted bread or flatbreads, as desired.

3 tbsp white vinegar

4 eggs

50g butter

20 curry leaves

1 tbsp olive oil

1 tsp ground paprika

1 tsp chilli flakes

½ tsp ground turmeric

1 tsp maple syrup

finely chopped mint leaves, to serve

toasted gluten-free bread or flatbreads (page 231), to serve

Saffron yoghurt

1 generous pinch saffron threads

210g unsweetened natural Greek yoghurt

1 clove garlic, finely minced or grated

2 tbsp freshly squeezed lemon juice

½ tsp sea salt

hands-on time	30 mins
total time	30 mins
serves	2

(VE) (GF)   (S)

Besan folds with apricot guac & crunchy bits

Apricot guac

flesh of 1 large avocado

¼ tsp sea salt

¼ tsp cracked black pepper

1 green chilli, finely chopped

1 handful coriander leaves, roughly chopped

freshly squeezed juice of ½ lime

¼ red onion, finely chopped

2 ripe apricots, pitted and chopped

Besan folds

1 tbsp cumin seeds

1 tsp coriander seeds

150g chickpea (besan) flour

1 tsp curry powder

2 tbsp finely chopped coriander

½ tsp sea salt

250ml milk (oat, soy or coconut)

1 tbsp coconut oil

To serve

1 tbsp coconut chips

1 tbsp pumpkin seeds

1 handful multi-coloured cherry tomatoes, sliced

fresh coriander leaves

lime wedges

Besan (chickpea) flour is lighter than wheat flour and has an excellent, earthy flavour. If fresh apricots are unavailable, you can easily substitute with tinned apricots, but using seasonal ingredients – avocados, herbs and tomatoes especially – is key to making this dish sing.

First make the apricot guac. Place the avocado flesh in a bowl and mash with a fork. Add the salt, pepper, chilli, coriander and lime juice and mix to combine. Stir through the onion and apricots and set aside.

For the besan folds, toast the cumin and coriander seeds in a large frying pan over medium heat, until fragrant. Use a mortar and pestle to grind to a coarse powder. Transfer to a medium-sized bowl. Add the chickpea flour, curry powder, coriander and salt and whisk to combine. Pour in the milk and whisk to a smooth, relatively thin batter. Set aside to rest for 5 minutes.

Heat half the coconut oil in the frying pan over medium-high heat, swirling to coat the base of the pan. Once hot, pour half the batter into the pan and tilt the pan a little so that it covers most of the base. Cook for 1–2 minutes, until bubbles start to form and pop in the centre. Turn over (you may need to work your way around the edge to loosen first) and cook for a further 1–2 minutes, until golden brown. Transfer to a plate and cover with a tea towel to keep warm. Add the remaining coconut oil to the pan and repeat with the remaining batter.

To serve, return the frying pan to medium heat, add the coconut chips and pumpkin seeds and toast for a couple of minutes until golden brown and the seeds are starting to pop. Transfer to a small bowl. Place the warm besan folds onto plates and spoon half the apricot guac into the centre of each. Top with the sliced tomato, crunchy bits, fresh coriander leaves and an extra squeeze of lime. Fold and devour.

hands-on time	1 hour
total time	3 hours 30 mins
makes	12 scrolls

 VE   S S A W

Dark chocolate, coconut & lime scrolls

Dough

250ml almond milk, heated until just warm

10g active dried yeast

40g caster sugar

110g coconut oil

50g soft brown sugar

450g high grade flour

5g sea salt

finely grated zest of 1 lime

Choc-coconut filling

50g coconut oil

50g tahini

100g desiccated coconut

100g soft brown sugar

200g vegan dark chocolate, roughly chopped

Lime glaze

150g icing sugar, sifted

freshly squeezed juice of 1 lime

50g coconut chips, toasted

The combination of chocolate and lime is one of my favourites, especially when coconut joins the party for a tropical lift.

To make the dough, whisk the warm almond milk, yeast and caster sugar in a small bowl. Leave in a warm place for 10–15 minutes, until frothy. Meanwhile, combine the coconut oil and brown sugar in a small saucepan and stir over low heat until the coconut oil has melted. Remove from the heat and set aside to cool a little. In a large bowl, whisk the flour, salt and lime zest. Make a well in the centre and pour in the yeast mixture and the oil and sugar mixture. Gently mix to form a soft, sticky dough. Transfer the dough to a clean work surface and knead for 10 minutes, until the dough is smooth and satiny. It will stick to your hands at first but try not to use any extra flour while kneading. Lightly oil the mixing bowl. Shape the dough into a ball and place into the bowl. Cover with clingfilm or a clean tea towel and leave in a warm place for about 1 ½ hours, or until doubled in size.

To prepare the filling, combine the coconut oil and tahini in a small saucepan. Stir over low heat until melted and smooth. Remove from the heat and set aside to cool a little. In a separate bowl, whisk the coconut and brown sugar to combine; set aside.

Shape the scrolls. Grease a large rectangular baking tin (33cm x 23cm) with oil and line with baking paper. Punch down the dough to remove the air and tip out onto a lightly floured surface. Roll the dough into a large rectangle, about 50cm x 30cm. Brush the surface of the dough evenly with the oil and tahini mixture. Sprinkle over the coconut and sugar mixture, then the chocolate. With a long side facing you, roll the dough into a tight log. Slice off the ends to neaten, then cut the log into 12 even pieces. Place the scrolls cut side up into the tin, spacing them evenly so they are almost touching. Cover loosely with a clean tea towel and leave for 1 hour in a warm place until risen and touching each other to fill the tin. Meanwhile, preheat the oven to 160°C fan-forced (or 180°C conventional).

Bake the scrolls for 25–30 minutes, until golden brown. Remove from the oven and leave to cool for 10 minutes.

To make the glaze, whisk the icing sugar and lime juice in a mixing bowl to form a smooth, thick glaze. Spoon the glaze over the warm scrolls and sprinkle with the coconut chips. Serve warm.

Note: To save time in the morning, you can do the initial dough prove in the fridge overnight. While the scrolls are best eaten fresh, you can store them in an airtight container for 2–3 days – just reheat in a low oven or in the microwave to serve.

Toasted coconut & chocolate porridge with balsamic cherries

hands-on time	10 mins
total time	10 mins
serves	2

(VE) S S A W

The combination of chocolate, cherry and coconut is like a warming bear hug in a bowl. Toasting the coconut brings out the nuttiness, maximising flavour.

To make the porridge, toast the desiccated coconut in a medium–large saucepan over medium heat for a few minutes, tossing occasionally, until golden brown. Add the oats, cocoa, cinnamon, maple syrup, milk and 250ml cold water. Bring to a simmer and cook for 5–6 minutes, until the oats have softened and thickened to a creamy porridge consistency.

For the balsamic cherries, place the ingredients into a small frying pan over medium heat. Cook for a few minutes, until the cherries are starting to soften and the liquid reduces to a syrup.

To serve, loosen the warm porridge with a little extra milk if necessary. Spoon into bowls and top with coconut yoghurt, balsamic cherries and toasted thread coconut.

35g desiccated coconut

100g rolled oats

1 ½ tbsp cocoa powder

½ tsp ground cinnamon

1 tbsp maple syrup

250ml non-dairy milk (oat, almond or coconut)

unsweetened natural coconut yoghurt, to serve

1 ½ tbsp thread coconut, toasted, to serve

Balsamic cherries

150g fresh or frozen cherries, pitted and halved

1 tbsp balsamic vinegar

1 tbsp maple syrup

Vegan hot cross buns

hands-on time	1 hour
total time	3 hours 30 mins
makes	12 buns

(VE)

These HCBs hit the mark. The tangzhong starter, a Japanese technique, makes the bread extra soft and stay fresh for longer. Ensure you use almond milk to activate the yeast, as other plant-based milks are less effective.

First make the tangzhong starter. Place the flour and water in a small saucepan and whisk until smooth. Cook over medium heat for a few minutes, stirring regularly, until thickened to a paste. Transfer to a small bowl and leave to cool to room temperature.

To prepare the sultanas, place in a bowl and cover with boiling water. Leave for 15 minutes until plump, then drain and leave to cool.

For the hot cross bun dough, whisk the warm almond milk, yeast and caster sugar in a small bowl. Leave for 10–15 minutes in a warm place until frothy. Combine the coconut oil, almond butter and brown sugar in a small saucepan over low heat. Stir for a couple of minutes until the almond butter has melted into the oil. Remove from the heat and leave to cool a little.

In a large bowl, sift together the flour, ground spices and salt then make a well in the centre. Pour the yeast mixture, almond butter mixture and tangzhong starter into the dry ingredients and gently mix to form a soft, slightly sticky dough. Transfer to a clean work surface and knead for 10 minutes, until the dough is soft, satiny and elastic. The dough will stick to your hands initially but avoid using any extra flour in the kneading process. Squeeze out any excess liquid from the sultanas and add to the dough with the grated orange zest, kneading until they are well mixed through. Form the dough into a large ball and return to the mixing bowl. Cover with clingfilm or a damp tea towel and leave in a warm place for 1 ½–2 hours, until doubled in size.

Grease a large rectangular baking tin (about 33cm x 23cm) with oil and line with baking paper.

Lightly push down the dough and divide into 12 pieces. On a clean surface, roll each piece of dough into a ball (by lightly pushing and turning the dough with the palm of one hand, cupping it slightly to form a ball). Place the balls into the tin, evenly spaced about 1cm apart (almost touching). Cover loosely with a tea towel and leave for 1–1 ½ hours in a warm place, until well risen and the balls are touching each other to fill the tin.

Meanwhile, preheat the oven to 160°C fan-forced (or 180°C conventional).

Tangzhong starter

| 25g high grade flour |
| 85ml cold water |

Dough

| 240g sultanas |
| 250ml almond milk, heated until just warm |
| 10g active dried yeast |
| 40g caster sugar |
| 75g coconut oil |
| 50g almond butter |
| 50g soft brown sugar |
| 450g high grade flour |
| 1 tbsp mixed spice |
| 1 tbsp ground cinnamon |
| 1 tsp ground ginger |
| 1 tsp ground cloves |
| 5g sea salt |
| finely grated zest of 1 orange |

Cross paste

| 85ml cold water |
| 85g plain flour |

Orange glaze

| 65g caster sugar |
| 60ml freshly squeezed orange juice |
| 2 tbsp boiling water |

To make the cross paste, whisk the water and flour together to make a reasonably thick but pipeable paste. Transfer the paste to a piping bag with a small round tip and pipe a thin cross onto each bun. Bake for 30 minutes, until a deep golden brown.

For the glaze, while the buns are baking, whisk the glaze ingredients in a small bowl or mug until the sugar has dissolved. As soon as they are removed from the oven, immediately brush the buns with the glaze so that the tops are glossy.

Serve while still slightly warm, or leave to cool to room temperature and serve lightly toasted, by themselves or with your favourite spread. Store in an airtight container.

Breakfast gözleme with preserved lemon mayo

hands-on time	1 hour 15 mins
total time	1 hour 15 mins
makes	6 gözleme

This gözleme recipe has been veganised, with potato and chickpeas the canvas for Turkish flavours of sumac, dill and mint. With a preserved lemon mayo, it's a zingy mouthful of goodness.

First make the gözleme dough. In a large bowl, sift together the flour, baking powder and sea salt. Whisk together the oil and 125ml cold water, then pour into the dry ingredients. Using your hands, bring together to form a rough dough. Knead the dough for a couple of minutes until smooth, wrap loosely with clingfilm, and set aside to rest in a warm place for 30 minutes.

For the filling, place the potatoes in a saucepan, cover with water and add 1 tsp of the salt. Bring to the boil over high heat and simmer vigorously for about 10 minutes, or until cooked through (a knife should go through each potato easily). Meanwhile, heat the olive oil in a large frying pan over medium heat. Add the onion and sauté for 8 minutes, until starting to soften. Add the cumin seeds, capsicum, spring onion, lemon zest, garlic, sumac, chilli flakes and dill. Cook for a further 3 minutes. Drain the potatoes well and add to the frying pan. Add the chickpeas and cook for 5 minutes over medium heat, roughly mashing up the potatoes and chickpeas as you go. Stir through the mint, lemon juice, remaining 1 ½ tsp salt and the pepper. It may seem like a lot of salt but the dough absorbs some of it as the gözleme cook. Transfer to a large bowl and leave to cool to room temperature.

Dough

300g high grade flour
1 ½ tsp baking powder
½ tsp sea salt
60ml olive oil
canola oil, for frying
sea salt flakes, to serve

Filling

500g agria potatoes, peeled and chopped into 3cm chunks
2 ½ tsp sea salt
2 tbsp olive oil
1 large red onion, thinly sliced
2 tsp cumin seeds
1 red capsicum, cored, deseeded and chopped into 2cm pieces
2 spring onions, finely chopped
finely grated zest and freshly squeezed juice of 1 lemon
4 cloves garlic, finely chopped
1 tbsp ground sumac
1 ½ tsp chilli flakes
1 tsp dried dill
400g can chickpeas, drained, aquafaba (liquid) reserved
2 tbsp finely chopped mint, plus extra to serve
½ tsp cracked black pepper

Preserved lemon mayo

60ml reserved aquafaba
½ tsp Dijon mustard
2 tsp lemon juice
2 cloves garlic, finely grated
185ml canola oil
skin of ½ preserved lemon (page 218), finely chopped
¾ tsp ground sumac
½ tsp cracked black pepper
sea salt, to taste

Meanwhile, for the preserved lemon mayo, place the aquafaba, mustard, lemon juice and garlic in a tall, narrow container. Using a stick blender, blitz for 20 seconds, until the aquafaba whitens and is becoming frothy. While continuing to blend, gradually pour in the oil, moving the stick blender up and down to emulsify. Gradually it will form a deliciously thick mayo. Add the preserved lemon, sumac and pepper. Blitz until smooth. Season to taste with salt – the preserved lemon is already a little salty so extra may not be necessary. Set aside.

To assemble the gözleme, divide the dough into six equal portions and roll into balls. On a lightly floured surface, roll one ball of dough to a circle 20–25cm in diameter (you want to roll it so thinly you can almost see through the dough). Spoon about 3 tbsp of the filling onto one half of the dough, leaving a 2cm border around the edge. Fold the other half of dough over the filling and push down around the edges to seal. Trim the edge to form an even half-circle, still with a 1–2cm border of dough enclosing the filling. Using a rolling pin, roll lightly towards the fold to flatten a little. Heat 1 tbsp canola oil in a large frying pan over medium heat. Once hot, add the gözleme to the pan and cook for 3 minutes on each side, until golden brown. Remove from the heat and transfer to a paper towel-lined plate. Repeat with the remaining dough and filling, assembling each gözleme as the one before is cooking. Add a little more oil to the pan before frying each one.

Serve the gözleme warm as they are cooked (or keep warm in a low oven while you cook them all), sprinkled with some sea salt flakes, chopped fresh mint and with the mayo for dipping.

Connect

Salads, sharing plates & street food

Connect is all about food that is made to share. I consider this chapter the heart of this book. The power of food is that it allows us to connect, not only to our friends and family but to the world.

A couple of years ago I went on a solo expedition to Tasmania, the picturesque island state of Australia. With its rugged coastline and lush mountains, it was the perfect spot for a week-long road trip and day-hike adventures. Being a foodie, no trip is ever complete without a little food tourism, and after seven days of hummus, nuts and soul-searching, I was ready to dive into the food scene in Hobart, Tasmania's capital. I had done some research and booked a table at a small neighbourhood restaurant, which celebrated seasonal and locally sourced produce. When I had gone to make my reservation online, I was faced with the proposition of booking a seat at my own table or choosing the 'communal dining' option, where you are seated at a shared table with others. While I'm not one to shy away from sitting at a restaurant on my own – I am THAT guy who takes himself to the movies – this 'communal' option sounded like a bit of fun.

That evening was one of the best dining experiences I've had. I was seated at a large round table with nine others: to one side a lawyer with an interest in local punk music and high fashion, to the other a woman who had tango danced her way across Europe and South America. Ten people with a shared passion for good food and good wine, but from wildly different backgrounds, different ages and different life experiences. As a stranger in a foreign city, the experience allowed me to connect to the land through the local produce and to the people and culture. The connection even extended beyond that evening – some of us met up the following night and still have links through social media.

All of the recipes in this chapter are best eaten with others. These are sharing plates perfect for family feasting, summer sessions with mates, potlucks and the like. It is food where everyone can dig in and enjoy to their heart's content. Some of these recipes are designed to be dissected as a group, while others encourage you to form an assembly line for group construction. Then there are some recipes that connect me to aspects of my own life, like the Gochujang beef & shiitake pizza (page 85), which combines my partner's true loves of bibimbap and Italian food in one delicious culinary collision.

I hope that the recipes in this chapter will become a part of both old and new connections with those you love.

Persimmon & red onion tarte Tatin with crispy sage & feta

hands-on time	35 mins
total time	1 hour
serves	6–8

This recipe showcases the sweet Fuyu persimmon in all its vibrant orange glory, paired with red onions, puff pastry, earthy sage and salty feta for a simple but show-stopping tart.

Preheat the oven to 180°C fan-forced (or 200°C conventional).

To make the filling, place a large ovenproof 24–26cm frying pan (such as cast iron) over medium heat. Pour in 2 tbsp of the olive oil and once hot, add the onions and sauté for 5 minutes. Add the garlic and chopped sage and cook for a further 3 minutes, until the onions are nicely softened and garlic is golden. Transfer to a bowl and set aside. Wipe the frying pan clean with paper towel, being careful as the pan will be hot.

Return the pan to medium-high heat and add the caster sugar to the centre of the pan. Heat for a few minutes, tilting the pan as the sugar melts, until it liquifies and forms a golden-brown caramel across the base. Add the butter, vinegar, salt and cinnamon and cook for a further two minutes, until the butter melts and the caramel is bubbling. Remove from the heat. Cut the top and bottom from the persimmons and slice into 3–5mm thick rounds (they don't need to be peeled). Place one slice in the centre of the pan then layer the remaining slices around, overlapping them a little so that they cover the caramel and the base of the pan. Scatter the onion mixture evenly over the persimmons.

To assemble, roll out the puff pastry on a lightly floured surface to about 5mm thick. Cut out a circle the same width as the top of the frying pan. Carefully place the pastry over the filling, tucking the edges down the sides of the pan. Using a fork, make a few holes in the pastry to allow steam to escape.

Bake for 30–35 minutes, until the pastry is puffed, crisp and golden brown. Remove from the oven and set aside for 5 minutes to cool slightly.

For the crispy sage, heat the remaining 2 tbsp olive oil in a small frying pan over medium-high heat. Add the sage leaves and fry for 30–60 seconds, until crispy. Use a slotted spatula to transfer to a paper towel-lined plate to drain.

To serve, carefully invert the tarte Tatin onto a large platter with a rim, as some of the caramel may flow from the tart. Top with the crispy sage leaves and crumbled feta. Serve warm.

4 tbsp olive oil

2 red onions, thinly sliced

2 cloves garlic, finely chopped

1 tbsp finely chopped sage leaves

150g caster sugar

50g butter

1 tbsp apple cider vinegar

½ tsp sea salt

½ tsp ground cinnamon

450g Fuyu persimmons (about 3)

400g rough puff pastry (page 229) or store-bought flaky puff pastry, thawed

16 whole sage leaves, extra

75g feta, crumbled

Showstopper cauli with speedy satay & hazelnut dukkah

hands-on time	35 mins
total time	40 mins
serves	6 as a side

(VE) (GF) S S A W

Not only is this delicious, it also looks beautiful – the parboiled and slightly charred cauli unfurling, with a spicy tahini satay, a sprinkling of dukkah and a flourish of chopped herbs. Made for sharing, place the cauli in the centre of the table and dig in together.

Preheat the oven to 220°C fan-forced (or 240°C conventional).

For the showstopper cauli, fill a large saucepan (big enough to fit your cauliflower) with water. Add 2 tbsp salt and bring to the boil over high heat. Carefully add the whole cauliflower and cook for about 8 minutes, until parboiled (a knife should go easily through most of the cauliflower but meet some resistance at the centre). In a bowl, whisk together the remaining cauli ingredients, including the remaining ½ tsp salt, to form a slightly runny paste. Drain the cauliflower and transfer to a rack to 'drip-dry' for 2 minutes. Transfer the cauliflower to a large casserole dish or roasting tin and brush the paste over, massaging it into the crevasses to evenly coat. Roast for 15 minutes, until the top of the cauliflower is slightly charred. Remove from the oven.

To make the speedy satay, place all ingredients into a jar or bowl. Add about 40ml cold water a little at a time, whisking with a fork after each addition until it forms a thick but pourable sauce.

For the hazelnut dukkah, toast the chopped hazelnuts in a dry frying pan over medium heat for 2–3 minutes, until just starting to brown a little. Add the cumin, coriander and sesame seeds and toast for a further 2 minutes, until the hazelnuts are golden brown and the seeds are fragrant and toasted. Use a mortar and pestle to grind until the seeds form a coarse powder around the chopped hazelnuts, still with some texture and crunch. Stir in the salt and pepper.

Serve the whole cauliflower hot, topped with the speedy satay, hazelnut dukkah and a generous sprinkling of coriander.

Showstopper cauli

2 tbsp + ½ tsp sea salt

1 large cauliflower, a few tender leaves left on

4 tbsp olive oil

finely grated zest and freshly squeezed juice of 1 lemon

1 tbsp muscovado sugar

1 tbsp ground sumac

1 tbsp ground cinnamon

1 tsp ground ginger

1 tsp ground cardamom

½ tsp ground chipotle chilli

3 tbsp finely chopped coriander, plus extra to serve

2 cloves garlic, finely chopped

½ tsp cracked black pepper

Speedy satay

3 tbsp crunchy peanut butter

1 tbsp tahini

freshly squeezed juice of ½ lemon

1 tbsp maple syrup

1 tsp gluten-free hoisin or gluten-free soy sauce

1 clove garlic, finely chopped

½ tsp ground chipotle chilli

¼ tsp sea salt

¼ tsp cracked black pepper

Hazelnut dukkah

40g hazelnuts, roughly chopped

1 ½ tsp each coriander seeds, cumin seeds and sesame seeds

½ tsp each sea salt and cracked black pepper

Portobello tacos with roasted cherry salsa & avocado cream

hands-on time	1 hour
total time	1 hour 15 mins
makes	16 tacos

(VE) (GF) S

These are like a party in your mouth – juicy mushrooms, a kicker salsa, creamy avocado and bangin' corn. If you have the time, I recommend making your own corn tortillas (page 228).

Preheat the oven to 180°C fan-forced (or 200°C conventional). If making your own corn tortillas, make the dough now.

For the marinated mushrooms, place the mushrooms and remaining ingredients in a bowl and toss to coat. Set aside for 20 minutes to marinate.

Meanwhile, for the roasted cherry salsa, place the cherries and tomatoes in a single layer in a roasting dish. Drizzle with the maple syrup and roast for 20 minutes, until softened. Meanwhile, heat the olive oil in a frying pan over medium heat. Add the onion and sauté for 5 minutes, until starting to soften. Add the garlic and chilli and cook for a further 2 minutes, until the garlic is turning golden. Transfer to a blender or food processor. Add the roasted cherries and tomatoes, lime juice, coriander and salt. Blitz until relatively smooth. Adjust to taste with extra salt or lime juice as desired.

If making your own corn tortillas, roll out and cook the tortillas now.

To cook the mushrooms, heat a large frying pan over medium-high heat. Remove the mushroom slices from the marinade and place in the hot pan in an even layer to fill the frying pan (you may need to cook the mushrooms in two batches). Cook for 4 minutes on each side until deeply browned, juicy and tender. Remove from the heat and cover to keep warm.

Meanwhile, to char the corn, bring a saucepan of water to the boil over high heat. Add the corn cobs and cook for 5 minutes. Drain and cool on a chopping board until you can handle them. Heat the mushroom frying pan over high heat. Stand the corn upright on the chopping board and use a sharp knife to cut off the kernels. Place the corn kernels in the frying pan and cook for a few minutes, until starting to char. Remove from the heat.

For the avocado cream, place all ingredients in a blender or food processor and blitz to a smooth, spreadable cream.

Marinated mushrooms

6 portobello mushrooms, stalks removed, cut into 1–2cm thick slices

4 tbsp olive oil

2 tbsp balsamic vinegar

2 tbsp gluten-free soy sauce

1 tbsp maple syrup

1 tsp ground chilli

1 tsp ground cumin

finely grated zest and freshly squeezed juice of 1 lime

Roasted cherry salsa

200g fresh or frozen cherries, pitted and halved

300g cherry tomatoes

1 tbsp maple syrup

2 tbsp olive oil

½ red onion, finely chopped

4 cloves garlic, finely chopped

1–2 long red chillies, finely chopped

freshly squeezed juice of 2 limes

1 small bunch (10g) coriander, leaves picked, plus extra to serve

1 tsp sea salt

Avocado cream

flesh of 2 ripe avocados

freshly squeezed juice of 1 lime

100ml coconut cream

¼ tsp sea salt

Additional ingredients

2 large corn cobs, husks and silk removed

16 small corn tortillas, homemade (page 228) or store-bought

To serve, gently warm the corn tortillas in a dry frying pan over medium-high heat for 15–30 seconds on each side. Stack and cover with a tea towel to keep warm. Spoon some of the avocado cream down the centre of each tortilla. Top with a couple of slices of mushroom, a generous spoonful of roasted cherry salsa, charred corn and extra coriander.

hands-on time	20 mins
total time	40 mins
serves	8–10 as a side

Ultra Brussels sprouts with apple, hazelnuts & feijoa dressing

- 800g Brussels sprouts, ends trimmed and outer leaves removed
- 1 green apple, cored, cut into thin matchsticks
- 1 large handful mint leaves, roughly chopped
- 4 tbsp olive oil
- ½ tsp sea salt
- ½ tsp cracked black pepper
- 70g hazelnuts, roughly chopped
- 4 cloves garlic, finely chopped
- 1 tbsp poppy seeds
- 1 tsp chilli flakes
- finely grated zest and freshly squeezed juice of 1 lime
- extra lime, to serve

Feijoa dressing

- flesh of 6 feijoas
- 1 green chilli, finely chopped
- finely grated zest and freshly squeezed juice of 2 limes
- 4 tbsp olive oil
- 3 tbsp coconut cream
- 1 tbsp maple syrup
- 1 tsp Dijon mustard
- 1 tsp cracked black pepper
- ½ tsp sea salt

Almost two dishes in one, here a zingy raw slaw combines with tender-roasted sprouts. The feijoa dressing really kicks through the slaw – but if these sweet, tangy fruit are unavailable you can use blitzed pears or extra citrus.

Preheat the oven to 190°C fan-forced (or 210°C conventional).

For the feijoa dressing, blitz all the ingredients in a blender or food processor until smooth and creamy.

Finely shred 400g of the Brussels sprouts, using a mandoline or sharp knife. Transfer to a large bowl and add the apple and mint. Pour the feijoa dressing over and toss to coat. Set aside for 30 minutes to allow the flavours to infuse.

Cut the remaining 400g Brussels sprouts in half lengthways and place into a roasting dish. Drizzle with 2 tbsp of the olive oil, season with the salt and pepper and toss to coat. Spread out to a single layer and roast for 10 minutes. Remove from the oven and add the hazelnuts in a single layer next to the sprouts. Reduce the oven to 160°C fan-forced (or 180°C conventional). Roast for 8 minutes, until the nuts are golden brown and the sprouts starting to crisp and char a little. Set aside.

Heat the remaining 2 tbsp olive oil in a large frying pan over medium heat. Add the garlic, poppy seeds and chilli flakes and cook for a couple of minutes, until the garlic is starting to turn golden. Add the roasted sprouts and hazelnuts, lime zest and juice to the pan and cook for 1 minute, tossing through to combine. Remove from the heat.

To serve, spoon the slaw onto the base of a large serving platter. Spoon the hot sprouts and hazelnuts over the top of the slaw. Squeeze over a little extra lime juice and serve immediately.

Walnut-sesame halloumi with chilli-caper capsicum & spring onion cannellini purée

hands-on time	30 mins
total time	30 mins
serves	4–6 as a side

(GF) (S) (S)

Crumbing halloumi can always get a little messy, but embrace it! The walnut and sesame crumb gives the halloumi a deliciously nutty crunch, which contrasts beautifully with the creamy purée.

First make the spring onion cannellini purée. Heat 2 tbsp olive oil in a large frying pan over medium–high heat. Add the spring onion and fry for 3 minutes, until starting to brown a little. Add the garlic and cook for 2 minutes, until the garlic is golden and parts of the spring onion are well-browned and starting to char. Transfer to a food processor, blender or a bowl with a stick blender. Add the remaining purée ingredients (including the remaining 4 tbsp olive oil) and blitz until relatively smooth, with the occasional streak of spring onion. Set aside.

For the chilli-caper capsicum, heat the oil in the same frying pan over medium heat. Add the capsicum, garlic, capers and chilli. Sauté for 4 minutes, until the capsicum is starting to soften and the garlic is golden brown. Transfer to a bowl and cover to keep warm.

For the walnut-sesame halloumi, you will need three shallow dishes. In the first dish, whisk the flour, cumin and pepper together with a fork. In the second dish, whisk the egg until the yolk and white become one. In the third dish, whisk the walnuts and sesame seeds together. Place the dishes near the stove top. Pat the halloumi slices dry with paper towel. Heat the oil in the frying pan over medium heat. Coat each piece of halloumi in the flour mixture, dip in the egg and then coat both sides with the walnut and sesame crumbs. This can be a little messy but get your hands in there. Place the crumbed halloumi in the frying pan and cook for 3–4 minutes on each side, until the coating is golden brown and crispy. Transfer the halloumi to a clean plate.

To serve, place the honey in a small saucepan over low heat and heat until runny. Spread the spring onion cannellini purée over the base of a large serving dish. Top with the chilli-caper capsicum, followed by the walnut-sesame halloumi. Sprinkle with the parsley and mint, give a generous squeeze of lemon juice and drizzle with the warm runny honey.

Cannellini purée

6 tbsp olive oil

4 spring onions, cut into 5cm pieces

3 cloves garlic, finely chopped

400g can cannellini beans, rinsed and drained

2 tbsp tahini

1 tbsp chopped flat-leaf parsley

finely grated zest and freshly squeezed juice of 1 lemon

1 tsp ground cumin

½ tsp sea salt

½ tsp cracked black pepper

Chilli-caper capsicum

2 tbsp olive oil

2 red capsicums, cored, deseeded and cut into 1cm slices

2 cloves garlic, finely chopped

1 tbsp capers

1 red birds-eye chilli, finely chopped

Walnut-sesame halloumi

3 tbsp flour (gluten-free or plain)

1 tsp ground cumin

½ tsp cracked black pepper

1 egg

60g walnuts, finely chopped

1 tbsp white sesame seeds

1 tbsp black sesame seeds

250g halloumi, cut into 1cm slices

2 tbsp canola oil

Additional ingredients

2 tbsp honey

3 tbsp finely chopped flat-leaf parsley leaves

1 handful mint leaves

generous squeeze of lemon juice

hands-on time	10 mins
total time	3 hours
	(+ overnight proving)
makes	1 large rectangular loaf

(VE)

Chilli, basil & olive overnight focaccia

450g high grade flour

1 sachet (8g) instant dried yeast

10g sea salt

2 tsp chilli flakes

2 tsp dried basil

50g pitted kalamata olives, drained and finely chopped

100ml olive oil, plus extra for drizzling

4 cloves garlic, finely chopped

coarse sea salt, to sprinkle

This no-knead focaccia could not be easier: mix (using instant dried yeast), put in the fridge, and the dough does the work overnight! While the method is simple, the bread is amazing – it still manages to achieve that bubbly, fluffy structure that you want in your focaccia. You can swap chilli, basil and olive for whatever's on hand – parsley, oregano and chopped sundried tomatoes for instance.

To make the focaccia dough, place the flour, yeast and salt in a large bowl, ensuring the salt is not touching the yeast. Pour in 410ml cold water and using your hands, mix to form a relatively wet dough (no kneading is required). Add the chilli flakes, basil, olives and 50ml of the olive oil, and mix through until just combined and evenly incorporated. Cover the bowl with clingfilm and refrigerate overnight (for a minimum of 12 hours and up to 24 hours).

Shape the focaccia. Generously oil a large rectangular baking tin (about 33cm x 23cm) with olive oil. Remove the dough from the fridge and bring the edges into the centre to deflate the dough. Tip the dough into the baking tin, folded side underneath, and using your hands, press out the corners of the dough, gently stretching to cover most of the base of the tin. Cover with clingfilm and leave in a warm place for about 2 ½ hours, until bubbly, wobbly and doubled in size.

While the dough is proving, mix the remaining 50ml olive oil and the garlic in a small bowl. Set aside to infuse for 2 hours.

Preheat the oven to 200°C fan-forced (or 220°C conventional).

To bake the focaccia, drizzle the garlic oil (including all the garlic) evenly over the dough. Use your fingers to press dimples all over the dough, reaching the bottom of the tin so that the oil pools in them (the dough will bounce back a little so you are left with dimples rather than holes). Sprinkle generously with coarse salt. Bake for 25–30 minutes, until golden brown and cooked through. Drizzle with extra olive oil, and carefully remove from the tin, using a spatula if needed. Serve warm or at room temperature.

Kūmara & tofu dumplings

hands-on time	1 hour
total time	1 hour 15 mins
makes	20 dumplings

(VE) S S A W

Simple to make and packed with goodness, I love stocking the freezer with these, ready to whip out at short notice when mates show up for dinner. Crumbled tofu gives a texture not dissimilar to pork mince. If garlic chives are hard to find, use ordinary chives and chopped fresh garlic.

Make the dipping sauce first to allow the flavours to infuse. Place all ingredients in a bowl, whisk together, then transfer to a shallow dish suitable for dipping. Set aside.

For the dumpling wrappers, use a wooden spoon or your hands to mix the flour and water in a bowl to make a firm but soft dough. It shouldn't be sticky. Knead a little until smooth, then form into a ball. Cover with clingfilm and leave to rest for 30 minutes.

For the filling, heat 2 tbsp of the canola oil in a large frying pan (that has a lid) or Dutch oven over medium heat. Add the tofu, cabbage and ginger and cook for 8 minutes, stirring occasionally, until the water released has fully evaporated and the cabbage is soft. Toss the kūmara, soy sauce, mirin and salt through and cook for a further 2 minutes, until the liquid is absorbed and any excess has evaporated. Transfer the mixture to a bowl, add the garlic chives and sesame oil and mix to combine. Season with salt to taste and set aside for 5 minutes to cool a little. You're better to slightly over-season, as the wrappers extract some of the salt as the dumplings cook. Clean the base of the frying pan with a paper towel.

To make the dumplings, divide the dough into 20 even portions (about 10g each), and roll into small balls. On a lightly floured work surface, take one piece of dough and roll out into a thin circle, 10cm in diameter. Place a heaped teaspoon of filling in the centre and fold the dough over to form a half-moon shape, pressing along the edge to close. Pinch and pleat the curved edges together to seal. Place onto a lightly floured tray, flat-side down, and cover with a damp tea towel to prevent drying out. Repeat with the remaining dough and filling to form 20 dumplings. You will have some leftover filling – it's delicious cooked and served on its own or stir-fried with noodles.

Heat the remaining 3 tbsp canola oil in the frying pan over medium-high heat. Add the dumplings, flat-side down, in a single layer (you may need to cook them in batches). Fry for 2 minutes (without touching them) until golden brown on the bottom, then pour in 60ml cold water and cover pan with a lid. Steam for 4 minutes, or until the water

Dipping sauce

4 tbsp light soy sauce

2 tbsp sesame oil

1 tbsp maple syrup

1 long red chilli, finely chopped

1 tbsp finely chopped coriander, plus extra to serve

Dumpling wrappers

150g high grade flour

80ml boiling water

Filling

5 tbsp canola oil, plus extra as needed

200g firm tofu, drained and crumbled

75g red cabbage, finely shredded

1 tbsp finely grated fresh ginger

1 small orange kūmara (about 300g), peeled and coarsely grated

2 tbsp light soy sauce

1 tbsp mirin

1 tsp sea salt

50g garlic chives, finely chopped

1 tbsp sesame oil

has evaporated. Remove the lid and fry for a further minute until the bottoms are crispy. Remove from the heat, and using a spatula transfer the cooked dumplings to a serving platter. Repeat until all of the dumplings are cooked (you will need to add more oil to the pan if cooking multiple batches).

Serve the dumplings hot, sprinkled with chopped coriander and with the dipping sauce.

Note: To freeze to cook later, assemble the dumplings, freeze on a tray until firm, then put in an airtight container. Cook as if fresh – no thawing required.

hands-on time	15 mins
total time	15 mins
serves	4–6 as a side

(VE) (GF)　　(S) (W)

Warm kale, chickpea & pomegranate salad with harissa yoghurt dressing

1 pomegranate

2 tbsp olive oil

½ red onion, thinly sliced

2 tsp poppy seeds

2 cloves garlic, finely chopped

50g almonds, roughly chopped

1 large bunch kale (about 250g), central stalks removed, leaves shredded

400g can chickpeas, rinsed and drained

Harissa yoghurt dressing

70g yoghurt (coconut or unsweetened natural)

2 tbsp apple cider vinegar

2 tsp rose harissa (page 217)

½ tsp sea salt

In this 'warm' salad, kale is lightly sautéed until just softened – retaining a little bite and structure but removing the bitterness and crunch it can have in its raw form.

First prepare the pomegranate. Roll the fruit on the benchtop, pressing to loosen the seeds. Cut the pomegranate in half and squeeze each half over a bowl to release about 2 tbsp juice. Set aside for the dressing. Cut each half in half (to create quarters), then with your thumbs on the back of each quarter, press and squeeze to release the seeds. Loosen out any remaining seeds with your fingers, removing any white pith that escapes into the bowl. Set the pomegranate seeds aside and discard the skins.

For the salad, heat the olive oil in a large, deep frying pan over medium heat. Add the onion and sauté for 5 minutes, until softened. Add the poppy seeds, garlic and almonds and fry for 3 minutes, until starting to brown a little. Add the kale and cook for 3 minutes, tossing regularly until the kale is just softened and a vibrant green. You may need to add the kale to the pan in two parts, adding more once the first lot has softened a little. Stir in the chickpeas and warm through for 1 minute. Transfer to a large mixing bowl. Add 4 tbsp of the pomegranate seeds and toss through.

For the harissa yoghurt dressing, place the yoghurt, apple cider vinegar, rose harissa, salt and 2 tbsp reserved pomegranate juice in a jar or bowl and mix to combine. Pour the dressing over the warm salad and toss through to coat. Transfer to a serving dish, sprinkle with a handful of extra pomegranate seeds and serve immediately.

Turmeric roast potatoes with crispy kawakawa & brown butter whip

hands-on time	30 mins
total time	1 hour 10 mins
serves	6–8 as a side

GF   S S A W

The perfect roast potato recipe, and potatoes this good deserve special treatment – kawakawa leaves, a plant endemic to Aotearoa, bring complexity to the brown butter and crisp up beautifully when fried to garnish. If kawakawa is unavailable, use fresh sage.

First start the brown butter whip. Melt the butter with the kawakawa leaves in a heavy-based saucepan over medium heat. Continue to cook for 3–5 minutes, stirring regularly and swirling the pan, until it starts to foam and the butter turns a deep golden brown (be careful here as it can rapidly go from brown to black). Pour the brown butter (including any flecks that have solidified) into a bowl, and discard the kawakawa leaves. Refrigerate the butter until cooled to the consistency of room temperature butter (this can take up to an hour). Stir a couple of times as it cools to mix up any browned solids with the melted butter. Remove from the fridge and set aside.

Preheat the oven to 190°C fan-forced (or 210°C conventional).

For the turmeric roast potatoes, pour the canola oil into a large roasting dish and place in the oven to heat. Place the potatoes in a large saucepan, cover with cold water and add 2 tbsp salt. Bring to the boil over high heat. Once boiling, parboil the potatoes by cooking for 5–10 minutes, until a knife can go easily through the outer edge of a potato but they are still firm in the centre. Drain then return to low heat and stir for 1 minute to dry out the potatoes a little. Remove from the heat and give the saucepan a decent shake until the edges of the potatoes are fluffed up. Add the sage and turmeric, tossing to coat. Carefully remove the roasting dish from the oven. Add the potatoes and carefully toss to coat with the hot oil. Roast for 35–40 minutes, until golden, crispy and cooked through. Remove from the oven and sprinkle with the pepper and remaining 1 tsp salt, tossing to coat.

To finish the brown butter whip, beat the brown butter with an electric hand mixer for 3 minutes until fluffy and whipped.

For the crispy kawakawa, place the olive oil in a small frying pan over medium-high heat. Once the oil is really hot, add the remaining kawakawa leaves and fry for 20–30 seconds on each side until blistered and crispy, then remove from the oil and place on a paper towel-lined plate to drain.

Serve the potatoes warm, topped with dollops of brown butter whip and the crispy kawakawa leaves.

Brown butter whip

150g butter, chopped into small cubes

6 kawakawa leaves

Turmeric roast potatoes

100ml canola oil

2kg agria potatoes, peeled and cut into 4cm chunks

1 tbsp + 1 tsp sea salt

1 tbsp finely chopped sage

2 tsp ground turmeric

½ tsp cracked black pepper

2 tbsp olive oil

8 kawakawa leaves

hands-on time	25 mins
total time	25 mins
serves	6 as a side

(VE) (GF) (S)

Cucumbers & tomatoes with pomegranate, tahini & za'atar

1 large telegraph cucumber (about 400g), quartered lengthways and cut into 1cm pieces

3 tbsp red wine vinegar

2 tbsp sesame oil

2 tbsp olive oil, plus extra to serve

1 tbsp maple syrup

¾ tsp sea salt

400g multi-coloured cherry tomatoes, halved

1 bunch mint, leaves picked and roughly chopped

1 bunch flat-leaf parsley, leaves picked and roughly chopped

3 tbsp tahini

1 tbsp pomegranate molasses

freshly squeezed juice of ½ lemon

Za'atar

1 tbsp cumin seeds

2 tbsp sesame seeds

1 tbsp ground sumac

1 tsp dried oregano

1 tsp dried thyme

½ tsp sea salt

This salad uses fresh seasonal produce to maximise flavour, with a lift of smooth pomegranate and tahini sauce and a generous sprinkling of za'atar, the Middle Eastern spice mix.

Marinate the vegetables. Combine the cucumber, vinegar, sesame oil, olive oil, maple syrup and salt in a large mixing bowl. Using your hands, massage the liquid into the cucumber. Add the tomatoes, mint and parsley. Toss gently together and set aside for 10 minutes for the marinade to meld with the juices from the vegetables.

For the za'atar, toast the cumin seeds in a frying pan over medium-high heat for a couple of minutes, until fragrant. Use a mortar and pestle to grind to a fine powder, then transfer to a small bowl. Toast the sesame seeds in the same pan until golden brown, then transfer to the bowl with the cumin. Add the sumac, oregano, thyme and salt. Mix to combine and set aside.

Drain 85ml of the juices from the cucumbers and tomatoes and place into a bowl. Add the tahini, pomegranate molasses and lemon juice and whisk to form a smooth sauce.

To serve, spoon the tahini sauce onto the base of a serving platter. Spoon the cucumbers and tomatoes onto the sauce, leaving behind any excess liquid. Sprinkle with a generous amount of za'atar (you will end up with some left over) and drizzle with a little extra olive oil. Serve immediately.

Springtime crostata with asparagus, kale, mint & ricotta

hands-on time	40 mins
total time	1 hour 55 mins
serves	6–8

Crostata is an Italian pastry tart, similar to a pie but freeform in nature, like a galette. Depending on the season, you could easily swap the asparagus for blanched broccoli, or kale for spinach.

First make the crostata pastry. In a large bowl, whisk together the flours and salt. Add the butter and use your hands to rub into the flour until it resembles coarse breadcrumbs – the odd coarser chunk of butter is okay. Add the apple cider vinegar then the iced water 1 tbsp at a time until the pastry dough just comes together to form a ball. Press down a little to form a thick disc, wrap loosely in clingfilm and refrigerate for 1 hour.

For the filling, heat the oil in a large frying pan over medium heat. Add the onion and sauté for 5 minutes, until starting to soften. Add the garlic and cumin, cook for 2 minutes, then stir in the kale, spring onion, half the lime juice, ½ tsp salt and ½ tsp pepper. Cook for 3 minutes, then add 60ml cold water. Cook for a further 5 minutes, until the water has evaporated and the kale is nicely wilted. Transfer to a large bowl and leave to cool to room temperature. Add the lime zest, remaining lime juice, ricotta, parmesan, mint and remaining salt and pepper. Stir until well combined, to form a thick creamy filling.

To prepare the asparagus, chop spears into 5cm and 10cm pieces. Place into a bowl and toss with the olive oil. Set aside.

Preheat the oven to 170°C fan-forced (or 190°C conventional).

To assemble the crostata, place a large sheet of baking paper on a clean surface and lightly sprinkle with flour. Roll the dough out on the baking paper to a 30cm round. Lift the baking paper and pastry onto a large oven tray. Sprinkle the ground almonds over the base of the pastry, leaving a 5cm border around the edge. Spoon the filling on top of the ground almonds and spread out with the back of a spoon to form an even layer. Arrange the asparagus pieces in a single layer on top of the filling in a geometric pattern and sprinkle with a little extra parmesan. Gently fold the pastry border over, pleating a little as you go, so that the edges of the filling are enclosed. Whisk the egg with 1 tbsp water and brush onto the folded pastry border. Bake for 40–45 minutes, until the pastry is golden brown.

To serve, set aside to cool for 5 minutes, then transfer to a serving platter or board. Sprinkle with extra chopped mint and serve warm or at room temperature.

Crostata pastry

150g plain flour, plus extra to sprinkle

75g spelt flour

½ tsp sea salt

150g chilled butter, cut into small cubes

1 tbsp apple cider vinegar

2–3 tbsp iced water

Filling

2 tbsp olive oil

1 red onion, thinly sliced

4 cloves garlic, finely chopped

2 tsp ground cumin

150g kale, central stalks removed, leaves finely shredded

1 spring onion, finely chopped

finely grated zest and freshly squeezed juice of 1 lime

1 tsp sea salt

1 tsp cracked black pepper

250g ricotta

50g finely grated parmesan, plus extra for topping

1 ½ tbsp chopped mint leaves, plus extra to serve

Additional ingredients

250g asparagus spears, woody ends trimmed

1 tbsp olive oil

4 tbsp ground almonds

1 egg

hands-on time	25 mins
total time	45 mins
	(+ overnight labneh)
serves	6 as a side

Roasted aubergines with cherry toms, tamarind sauce & sesame labneh

Here, tender aubergine meets blistered sweet tomatoes, creamy nutty labneh, and tangy sauce. Buy a piece of cheesecloth from a craft or kitchen store, even if it's just for making this labneh, it's worth it.

Sesame labneh

500g yoghurt (coconut or unsweetened natural Greek)

½ tsp sea salt

2 tbsp olive oil

1 tbsp tahini

finely grated zest of ½ lemon

Roasted aubergines & cherry toms

2 medium–large aubergines (about 600g total), sliced into 1cm rounds

250g cherry tomatoes

60ml olive oil

½ tsp sea salt

½ tsp cracked black pepper

Tamarind sauce

1 ½ tbsp tamarind paste

1 tbsp freshly squeezed lemon juice

1 tbsp finely grated fresh ginger

2 cloves garlic, finely chopped

1 tsp maple syrup (or honey if non-vegan)

½ tsp sea salt

¼ tsp ground chilli

Additional ingredients

1 tbsp sesame seeds

1 large handful flat-leaf parsley leaves, roughly chopped

Prepare the sesame labneh a day ahead. Place the yoghurt and salt in a bowl and mix to combine. Line a sieve with doubled cheesecloth and set over a bowl. Pour the salted yoghurt into the cheesecloth, fold the corners over to cover and place a gentle weight (such as a mug or a block of butter) on top. Place in the fridge for 24 hours (or up to 3 days) to allow some liquid to strain from the yoghurt.

Preheat the oven to 200°C fan-forced (or 220°C conventional). Line 2 large oven trays with baking paper.

To roast the aubergines and cherry tomatoes, place the aubergine rounds and cherry tomatoes onto the oven trays in a single layer. Brush both sides of each aubergine round with a generous amount of olive oil then drizzle the remaining oil over the cherry tomatoes. Season with salt and pepper. Roast for 30 minutes, turning the aubergine rounds over halfway through, until tender and the tomatoes are starting to blister. Remove from the oven and leave to cool for 5 minutes.

For the tamarind sauce, place 6 of the roasted cherry tomatoes and the remaining ingredients with 4 tbsp water in a bowl and blitz with a stick blender (or use a blender) until relatively smooth. Set aside.

To finish the sesame labneh, bring the corners of the cheesecloth together and twist to squeeze out any extra liquid. Transfer the thickened yoghurt to a bowl and add the olive oil, tahini and lemon zest, mixing until smooth.

To serve, toast the sesame seeds in a frying pan over medium-high heat for 2–3 minutes, stirring occasionally, until fragrant and starting to brown a little. Remove from the heat and set aside. Spoon the sesame labneh onto the base of a large serving platter, spreading it out into a large disc with the back of a spoon. Arrange the roasted aubergine slices on the labneh then scatter over the cherry tomatoes. Spoon dollops of the tamarind sauce over the vegetables. Sprinkle with the sesame seeds and parsley. Serve warm or at room temperature.

Killer beans with lemongrass, cashews & kaffir lime

hands-on time	15 mins
total time	15 mins
serves	6 as a side

(VE) (GF)

This recipe was inspired by a killer crop of green beans one summer. Serve as a flavour-bomb side dish for your next shared meal, or with tofu, chicken or noodles for a speedy main. If Thai basil is not available, use coriander leaves or Vietnamese mint.

Preheat the oven to 160°C fan-forced (or 180°C conventional). Line a small oven tray with baking paper.

First roast the cashews. Place the cashews on the oven tray in a single layer. Roast for 10 minutes, until golden. Set aside.

For the beans, bring a large saucepan of water to the boil over high heat. Add the beans and cook for 2 minutes, then drain and rinse under cold water to refresh and stop the cooking process. Use a mortar and pestle to grind the lemongrass, garlic, ginger, kaffir lime leaves and chilli flakes to a rough, chunky paste. Melt the coconut oil in a large frying pan over medium-high heat. Add the paste and cook for 1 minute, moving around the pan to evenly fry. Add the green beans, soy sauce, maple syrup and salt. Cook for a further 2 minutes, tossing the beans with the paste to evenly coat and heat through. Remove from the heat and add the lime juice, Thai basil and roasted cashews, tossing evenly through the beans.

To serve, use tongs to pile the beans and cashews on a serving dish. Pour over any remaining liquid and delicious bits left in the pan. Serve warm or at room temperature.

110g cashews

500g green beans, ends trimmed

2 stalks lemongrass, tough outer layers removed, ends trimmed, finely chopped

4 cloves garlic, finely chopped

1 tbsp finely grated fresh ginger

2 kaffir lime leaves, thinly sliced

1 tsp chilli flakes

2 tbsp coconut oil

2 tbsp gluten-free light soy sauce

1 tbsp maple syrup

½ tsp sea salt

2 tbsp freshly squeezed lime juice

1 large handful Thai basil leaves, roughly chopped

Olive tapenade & feta star bread

hands-on time	50 mins
total time	3 hours 15 mins
makes	1 large star bread

 S S A W

Bread is made to be shared. In this recipe, discs of dough are rolled out, layered with a punchy olive and feta filling, then cut and twisted into a star shape for tearing-and-sharing.

First make the tangzhong starter. Place the flour and milk in a small saucepan and whisk until smooth. Cook over medium heat for a few minutes, stirring regularly, until thickened to a paste. Transfer to a small bowl and leave to cool to room temperature.

For the dough, whisk the flour, sugar, salt and yeast (don't place the yeast directly on top of the salt) in a large bowl. Make a well in the centre, add the tangzhong starter and 185ml cold water and mix to a soft dough. Tip the dough out onto a clean work surface, add the butter and knead for 10–15 minutes until the dough is smooth and elastic. Add the oregano and knead into the dough until well dispersed. Roll the dough into a ball, lightly grease the mixing bowl with oil and return the dough to the bowl. Cover the bowl with a damp tea towel and leave in a warm place for 1 ½ hours, until doubled in size.

For the tapenade, place all the ingredients, except the feta, in a food processor or blender and blitz to form a paste. Set aside.

Tangzhong starter

25g high grade flour

85ml milk

Dough

375g high grade flour

40g caster sugar

8g sea salt

1 sachet (8g) instant dried yeast

75g butter, softened to room temperature, chopped

1 tbsp dried oregano

Olive tapenade & feta filling

150g pitted black or kalamata olives

2 tbsp capers

3 cloves garlic, finely chopped

finely grated zest and freshly squeezed juice of ½ lemon

3 tbsp finely chopped flat-leaf parsley leaves

1 ½ tsp ground cumin

¾ tsp ground coriander

½ tsp ground chilli

60ml olive oil

150g feta, crumbled

Additional ingredients

1 egg

sea salt flakes, to sprinkle

To assemble the star bread, line a large oven tray with baking paper and dust the paper with a little flour. Knock down the dough to release the air and divide into four equal pieces. Dust a work surface lightly with flour and roll out the first portion of dough into a large thin disc, about 25cm in diameter. Transfer the disc to the oven tray and spread one third of the olive tapenade over, leaving a 2cm border without filling. Sprinkle over one third of the feta. Roll out the next piece of dough to the same size. Carefully place the disc on top of the filling and spread with half the remaining olive tapenade and feta. Repeat with the third piece of dough and remaining tapenade and feta. Roll out and place the final disc of dough on top. Mark (without cutting) an 8cm diameter circle in the centre, or place an 8cm bowl or cup in the centre. Cut the layered disc into sixteen even pieces, stopping at the marked circle so the centre remains intact. Take two pieces and twist them outwards from each other a few times before joining the ends together to seal. Repeat with the remaining pieces to create an eight-pointed star. Trim the points so they are even in length with nicely pointed ends. Cover loosely with clingfilm and leave in a warm place for 30 minutes to rise a little.

Meanwhile, preheat the oven to 160°C fan-forced (or 180°C conventional).

To bake the bread, whisk the egg and 1 tbsp water together then brush evenly onto the star. Sprinkle with sea salt flakes. Bake for 30–35 minutes, until golden brown and baked through. Remove from the oven and leave to cool before transferring to a board.

Serve the bread warm or at room temperature. Tear and share.

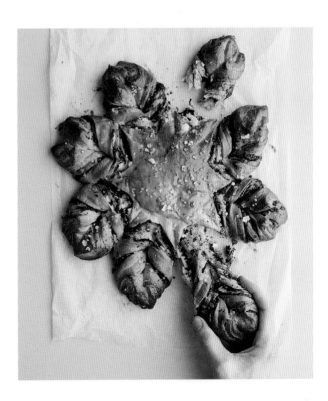

hands-on time	20 mins
total time	40 mins
serves	6 as a side

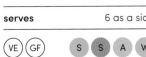

Roasted brassica & lentil salad with orange cream & chilli oil

Chilli oil

60ml canola oil

1 tbsp chilli flakes

2 cloves garlic, finely chopped

finely grated zest of 1 orange

Roasted brassicas & lentils

4 tbsp olive oil

1 tsp ground cumin

1 tsp ground coriander

1 tsp amchur

1 tbsp finely grated fresh ginger

½ tsp sea salt

½ tsp cracked black pepper

½ cauliflower, chopped into medium florets

1 head broccoli, chopped into medium florets

400g can lentils, rinsed and drained

1 spring onion, cut into 1cm slices

70g almonds, roughly chopped

1 tbsp sage leaves, finely chopped

Orange cream

400ml can coconut cream, refrigerated overnight

60ml freshly squeezed orange juice

1 tbsp apple cider vinegar

pinch of sea salt

This is excellent as a hearty vegan side or a winter salad to share. Amchur, a citrusy powder made from dried unripe green mangoes, can be found at Indian or Asian food stores. Make sure you refrigerate the can of coconut cream a day in advance, ready for the orange cream.

Preheat the oven to 190°C fan-forced (or 210°C conventional).

First make the chilli oil. Place the oil in a small saucepan over medium heat and warm for 5 minutes. Remove from the heat and stir through the chilli flakes, garlic and orange zest. Cover with a lid and set aside to allow the flavours to infuse into the oil for a minimum of 30 minutes (the longer the better).

For the roasted brassicas & lentils, whisk the olive oil, cumin, coriander, amchur, ginger, salt and pepper in a large bowl. Add the cauliflower and broccoli and toss to coat. Transfer to 2 oven trays and spread out in a single layer. Roast for 15 minutes. Remove from the oven and add the lentils, spring onion, almonds and sage, dividing evenly between each tray. Toss to combine. Return to the oven and roast for a further 10 minutes, until the brassicas are tender and the almonds are turning golden brown. Set aside for a couple of minutes to cool slightly.

To make the orange cream, scoop 200ml of the solidified coconut cream from the chilled can into a bowl. Stir in the orange juice, apple cider vinegar and salt. Gently swirl 2 tbsp of the chilli oil into the cream.

To serve, spread the orange cream across the base of a large serving dish. Pile the roasted brassicas and lentils on top of the cream and drizzle over the remaining chilli oil (including the garlic and orange zest).

hands-on time	15 mins
total time	45 mins
serves	4–6 as a side

(GF)

Zhug prawn salad with watermelon & feta

Zhug

10 green cardamom pods
1 tsp cumin seeds
1 tsp coriander seeds
1 tsp whole black peppercorns
4 cloves garlic, finely chopped
4 green chillies, finely chopped
1 tsp sea salt
1 bunch (20g) coriander, leaves picked
1 bunch (20g) flat-leaf parsley, leaves picked
125ml olive oil
finely grated zest and freshly squeezed juice of 1 lemon

Salad

300g raw jumbo prawns, peeled and deveined, tails intact
1 tbsp olive oil
800g watermelon flesh (about ½ a medium-sized watermelon), chopped into large chunks
½ red onion, thinly sliced
freshly squeezed juice of 1 lime
1 small bunch mint, leaves picked and roughly chopped
100g feta, crumbled

The hero of this salad is the zhug, a green Yemeni hot sauce used here to marinate juicy prawns. It gives a decent kick that's balanced nicely by cooling watermelon, fresh mint and salty feta. This recipe is easily made vegetarian by swapping prawns for halloumi.

First make the zhug. Use a mortar and pestle to bash the cardamom pods to release the seeds. Discard the pods. Toast the cardamom, cumin and coriander seeds and peppercorns in a frying pan over medium heat for a minute or two, until fragrant. Use the mortar and pestle to grind the toasted spices to a fine powder. Add the garlic, chillies and salt and pound to form a rough paste. Add the herbs a little at a time, continuing to pound to form a chunky paste. To finish, gradually add the olive oil while stirring to emulsify and finally stir through the lemon zest and juice. You will make more than needed for the salad – store leftover zhug in the refrigerator for up to 5 days.

To cook the prawns, place the prawns and 4 tbsp of zhug in a bowl and toss to coat evenly. Refrigerate for 30 minutes to marinate. Heat the olive oil in a large frying pan over medium-high heat. Add the prawns with the marinade and cook, tossing occasionally, for 3–4 minutes, until the prawns change colour and are cooked through. Remove from the heat.

To prepare the watermelon, place the watermelon, red onion, lime juice and half the chopped mint in a bowl. Using your hands, toss to coat, massaging the red onion into the juices to soften it slightly.

Arrange the watermelon mixture on a large serving platter. Top with the feta, prawns (with any zhug juices from the pan), and remaining chopped mint.

Note: To make this recipe vegetarian, substitute the prawns with 300g halloumi. Cut into 1cm thick slices and marinate with the zhug as you would the prawns. In a large frying pan over medium-high heat with the oil, cook for 3 minutes on each side until golden.

Baba ganoush with syrupy figs & walnuts

hands-on time	15 mins
total time	1 hour 40 mins
serves	6 as a side

(VE) (GF) S A

The secret to baba ganoush is in charring the aubergines' skin to give the flesh a smoky flavour. My recipe uses an oven grill to achieve a similar char to an open-flame stovetop, meaning you don't smoke up your kitchen in the process. The marriage of this creamy aubergine dip with caramelised figs and walnuts is pure heaven, and well worth the effort.

Preheat the oven on the fan-grill function to HIGH. Line an oven tray with foil.

First, cook the aubergines. Pierce each aubergine in a couple of places with a sharp knife and place onto the oven tray. Place the tray in the top half of the preheated oven and grill for 1 hour, using tongs to turn 2 or 3 times, until they are evenly charred and the flesh is soft enough so that they are starting to collapse. Set aside until cool enough to handle. Cut in half, scoop out the flesh and place in a sieve set over a bowl. Set aside for 30 minutes to allow any excess liquid to drain.

To roast the figs and walnuts, change the oven function to bake and preheat to 160°C fan-forced (or 180°C conventional). Line an oven tray with baking paper. Arrange the figs cut side up on the oven tray. Whisk the maple syrup, pomegranate molasses and balsamic vinegar together. Drizzle over the figs and season with a little sea salt and black pepper. Roast for 10 minutes. Remove from the oven, scatter the walnuts around the figs and return to the oven for a further 10 minutes, until the walnuts are turning golden and the figs are caramelised.

To make the baba ganoush, transfer the drained aubergine flesh to a bowl. Add the lemon zest, juice, garlic, tahini, olive oil, salt, pepper and 2 tbsp of the parsley. Stir together with a fork, gently mashing the aubergine to make a slightly chunky but creamy texture. Adjust seasoning to taste.

To serve, spoon the baba ganoush into a wide bowl or plate with a rim and spread out with the back of a spoon. Arrange the roasted figs and walnuts in the centre, drizzle over any of the remaining syrup from the figs and a little extra olive oil. Sprinkle with the remaining chopped parsley and serve with your favourite bread for dipping.

1kg aubergines (about 2 large or 3 medium)

6–8 fresh figs, stalks removed, halved

2 tbsp maple syrup

1 tbsp pomegranate molasses

1 tbsp balsamic vinegar

50g walnuts, roughly chopped

finely grated zest and freshly squeezed juice of 1 lemon

2 cloves garlic, finely grated

3 tbsp tahini

3 tbsp olive oil, plus extra for drizzling

¾ tsp sea salt, or to taste

½ tsp cracked black pepper

3 tbsp roughly chopped flat-leaf parsley leaves

Pearl couscous salad with preserved lemon, cherries & pistachios

hands-on time	20 mins
total time	30 mins
serves	6 as a side

This recipe is a little bit of fun, with pops of colour from the cherries and pistachios among the beads of couscous. The preserved lemon picks up the Dijon mustard in the dressing so that they soar together.

Preheat the oven to 160°C fan-forced (or 180°C conventional). Line a small oven tray with baking paper.

First cook the pearl couscous. Finely chop half the red onion – you will use the other half later. Heat the olive oil in a saucepan over medium heat. Add the chopped onion and sauté for 5 minutes, until starting to soften. Add the couscous, garlic and orange zest and cook for 2 minutes to toast a little. Pour in the stock, orange juice and 250ml water. Increase the heat to high and bring to the boil, then reduce the heat to medium and simmer for 10–12 minutes, stirring occasionally, until the couscous is cooked and most of the liquid is absorbed. Remove from the heat, drain off any excess liquid, and transfer to a bowl to cool a little.

Meanwhile, place the pistachios onto the oven tray in a single layer and roast for 10 minutes, until fragrant. Transfer to a bowl and set aside to cool.

For the dressing, place all the ingredients in a jar, seal tightly with a lid and shake together until well combined. Adjust seasoning to taste and set aside to allow the flavours to infuse.

To make the salad, thinly slice the remaining red onion half. Add to the couscous with the cherries, mint, parsley, spinach and dressing, tossing to combine. Transfer to a serving bowl and set aside for 10 minutes to allow the flavours to infuse. To finish, roughly chop the roasted pistachios and sprinkle over the salad, along with some extra chopped mint and parsley.

1 red onion, halved

2 tbsp olive oil

300g pearl (Israeli) couscous

2 cloves garlic, finely chopped

finely grated zest of 1 orange

375ml vegetable stock

60ml freshly squeezed orange juice

50g pistachio kernels

200g fresh cherries, pitted and halved

1 large handful mint leaves, roughly chopped, plus extra to serve

1 large handful flat-leaf parsley leaves, roughly chopped, plus extra to serve

75g spinach leaves, shredded

Dressing

60ml olive oil

2 tbsp red wine vinegar

1 tbsp maple syrup

1 tsp Dijon mustard

freshly squeezed juice of ½ lemon

skin of ½ preserved lemon, finely chopped

½ long red chilli, finely chopped

sea salt, to taste

hands-on time	1 hour 15 mins
total time	1 hour 15 mins
makes	12 bao

(VE) S S A W

Five spice tofu bao with sesame-orange sauce, pickles & sticky cashews

Sticky cashews

150g cashews

1 tbsp maple syrup

1 tbsp sesame oil

½ tsp each of sea salt and cracked black pepper

Sesame-orange sauce

1 tbsp sesame oil

4 cloves garlic, finely chopped

1 tbsp finely grated fresh ginger

2 tsp black sesame seeds

finely grated zest of 1 orange

60ml freshly squeezed orange juice

4 tbsp dark soy sauce

2 tbsp mirin

2 tbsp apple cider vinegar

2 tbsp maple syrup

¼ tsp each of sea salt and cracked black pepper

¼ tsp ground chilli

Five spice tofu

600g firm tofu, drained

75g cornflour

2 tsp ground Chinese five spice

½ tsp each of sea salt and cracked black pepper

4 tbsp canola oil

To assemble

12 steamed bao (page 226)

quick-pickled cucumber (page 219)

coriander onions (page 219)

Thai basil or Vietnamese mint leaves

These vegan bao are great for feasting with friends. Frying the tofu for 4 minutes on each side ensures the five-spice coating gets extra crispy, bringing crunch to counter the soft texture of the bun. The sesame-orange sauce pops, the sticky cashews crackle and the pickles zing.

Preheat the oven to 160°C fan-forced (or 180°C conventional). Line an oven tray with baking paper.

For the sticky cashews, place all the ingredients in a bowl and stir to coat the cashews. Tip the cashews and coating onto the oven tray and spread to a single layer. Roast for 10 minutes, until golden brown. Transfer the cashews and any sticky bits to a board, cool slightly, then roughly chop. Set aside.

To make the sesame-orange sauce, heat the sesame oil in a saucepan over medium heat. Add the garlic, ginger and black sesame seeds and fry for 2 minutes, until just starting to brown. Add the remaining ingredients, increase the heat to medium-high and bring to the boil. Cook for 5 minutes until the sauce has reduced a little and is dark amber in colour. Transfer to a bowl and set aside to cool completely (the sauce will thicken a little more as it cools).

For the five spice tofu, cut the tofu slab into twelve slices about 1.5cm thick. Pat dry on both sides with a doubled-over paper towel, then leave on a paper towel-lined plate for 10 minutes to remove some of the extra moisture. In a shallow bowl, whisk together the cornflour, five spice, salt and pepper. Heat the oil in a large frying pan over medium-high heat. Coat each piece of tofu in the cornflour and shallow-fry for about 4 minutes each side, until crispy and golden brown. Depending on the size of your pan, you may need to do this in two batches. Remove from the pan and place on a paper towel-lined plate to drain any excess oil.

Assemble the bao. Fill the warm steamed buns with a slab of five spice tofu, sesame-orange sauce (including all the chunky bits), pickled cucumber, coriander onions, Thai basil or Vietnamese mint leaves and a sprinkling of sticky cashews.

Note: Make the bao dough in advance and steam close to serving so the buns are warm when eating.

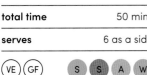

hands-on time	20 mins
total time	50 mins
serves	6 as a side

(VE) (GF) S S A W

Citrus-roasted broccolini with hazelnut romesco, rocket & mint

Maple-roasted hazelnuts

140g hazelnuts, roughly chopped

3 tbsp maple syrup

¼ tsp sea salt

Hazelnut romesco

2 red capsicums, cored, deseeded and cut into quarters

3 tbsp olive oil

2 tbsp tomato paste

1 tbsp balsamic vinegar

1 tsp ground paprika

½ tsp sea salt

½ tsp cracked black pepper

¼ tsp ground cinnamon

2 cloves garlic, finely chopped

1 tbsp chopped oregano

Citrus-roasted broccolini

400g broccolini

finely grated zest and freshly squeezed juice of ½ orange

finely grated zest and freshly squeezed juice of ½ lemon

2 tbsp olive oil

Additional ingredients

1 large handful rocket leaves

1 handful mint leaves

My favourite way to cook broccolini is roasting it, just enough to give it a little char and soften it slightly. Citrus goes well here to give it some oomph, and it's the hazelnut romesco that you'll be coming back to time and time again. This shines as part of a shared feast with friends, particularly alongside fish or lamb.

Preheat the oven to 160°C fan-forced (or 180°C conventional). Line 2 oven trays with baking paper.

First make the maple-roasted hazelnuts. Place the hazelnuts in a single layer on one oven tray. Drizzle with maple syrup and sprinkle with salt. Roast for 12 minutes, until golden brown. Set aside to cool. Increase the oven temperature to 200°C fan-forced (or 220°C conventional).

Roast the capsicums for the hazelnut romesco. Place the capsicums on the second oven tray and roast for 25 minutes, until soft and starting to blister and char a little. Set aside to cool slightly.

Meanwhile, for the citrus-roasted broccolini, place the broccolini in a single layer in a large roasting dish. Sprinkle with the orange and lemon zest, squeeze over the orange and lemon juice, and drizzle with the olive oil. Add to the oven (at the same time as the capsicums) and roast for 15 minutes, until the broccolini is just tender and starting to char a little.

For the hazelnut romesco, place the roasted capsicums, two-thirds of the maple-roasted hazelnuts and all remaining romesco ingredients in a food processor and blitz to form a relatively thick and slightly chunky sauce.

To serve, lay the roasted broccolini on a serving platter, spoon over the hazelnut romesco, then top with the rocket and mint. Sprinkle with the remaining maple-roasted hazelnuts. Serve warm or at room temperature.

Grilled sweetcorn & nectarine salad with miso dressing

hands-on time	20 mins
total time	20 mins
serves	6 as a side

(VE) (GF)   S

This fresh and vibrant salad will light up your outdoor summer spread. It's best cooked on the hot barbecue grill, but the sweetcorn, spring onion, and nectarines can easily be grilled in a frying pan over medium-high heat. Just ensure you use a little oil if grilling on the stovetop.

For the salad, heat a barbecue grill until hot. Barbecue the corn for 10–15 minutes, turning occasionally, until most of the corn kernels are lightly charred. At the same time, barbecue the spring onion for 5–10 minutes, until browned and starting to char a little. Transfer the spring onion to a large bowl. Transfer the corn to a chopping board. Once cool enough to handle, stand the corn upright, and use a small sharp knife to cut off the kernels. Add the corn to the bowl with the spring onions and discard the cobs.

Place the nectarine wedges on the barbecue and grill for 3 minutes, turning to cook both sides, until browned and softened a little. Add the grilled nectarine to the bowl, along with the basil and cucumber.

For the miso dressing, place all the ingredients in a bowl and whisk until smooth. Pour the dressing over the warm salad and toss through to coat. Transfer to a serving dish. This salad is best served warm, but is happily refrigerated and eaten cold the following day.

Salad

4 large corn cobs, husks and silks removed

6 spring onions, cut into 5cm pieces

4 nectarines, stones removed, sliced into 1cm wedges

1 large handful basil leaves, torn

1 telegraph cucumber (about 300g), quartered lengthways and cut into 1cm dice

Miso dressing

3 tbsp maple syrup

1 ½ tbsp shiro (white) miso paste

freshly squeezed juice of 2 lemons

½ long red chilli, finely chopped

6 tbsp olive oil

hands-on time	30 mins
total time	1 hour 30 mins
makes	2 large pizzas

Gochujang beef & shiitake pizza

Pizza toppings and base

250g premium beef mince

2 tbsp sesame oil, plus extra to serve

2 tbsp soy sauce

1 tbsp maple syrup

3 cloves garlic, finely chopped

20g dried sliced shiitake mushrooms

2 tbsp canola oil

⅔ quantity two-hour pizza dough (page 224), see note

2 handfuls baby spinach leaves

2 eggs

mung bean sprouts, to serve

Gochujang pizza sauce

1 tbsp sesame seeds

4 tbsp gochujang paste

2 tbsp sesame oil

2 tbsp rice wine vinegar

1 tbsp soy sauce

1 tbsp maple syrup

2 cloves garlic, finely chopped

For this pizza, which plays off the flavours of Korean bibimbap, you'll need to make the two-hour pizza dough in advance (page 224, and see note below). You can substitute dried shiitake for any fresh mushroom; just skip the soaking and adjust amounts as needed.

Prepare the pizza toppings. Place the beef mince, sesame oil, soy sauce, maple syrup and two-thirds of the garlic in a bowl. Mix to combine and refrigerate for 1 hour to allow the mince to marinate. Place the dried shiitake mushrooms in a bowl, cover with hot water and leave for 30 minutes until softened.

Preheat the oven to 230°C fan-forced (or 250°C conventional). Place 2 pizza stones (or oven trays) in the oven as it heats – this will ensure your pizzas have a crispy base.

Drain the mushrooms and pat dry with paper towel. Remove any stalks. Heat 1 tbsp of canola oil in a large frying pan over medium heat. Add the mushrooms and sauté with the remaining garlic for 3 minutes, until the garlic is golden brown. Transfer to a bowl, season with a little sea salt and cracked black pepper and set aside. Heat the remaining oil in the frying pan over medium-high heat. Add the beef and cook for 5 minutes, stirring occasionally, until browned. Drain any excess liquid from the pan, and set the beef aside.

For the gochujang pizza sauce, toast the sesame seeds in a small frying pan over medium heat for a couple of minutes, until golden brown. Transfer to a bowl, add the remaining sauce ingredients, and mix to form a paste.

To assemble the pizzas, shape the dough (using the instructions in the two-hour pizza dough recipe), so that you have two large pizza bases. Place these on two sheets of baking paper. Spoon half the gochujang sauce onto each base and spread out evenly with the back of a spoon. Top with the beef, shiitake mushrooms and some baby spinach leaves. Remove one of the hot pizza stones from the oven and transfer one pizza on the baking paper onto the hot stone. Bake for 10 minutes then remove from the oven and crack one egg into the centre of the pizza. Return to the oven and bake for a further 3–5 minutes, until the base is crispy and the egg is cooked but the yolk is still a little runny. Drizzle with extra sesame oil and sprinkle with mung bean sprouts. Cut into slices and serve hot. Repeat, using the second pizza stone to bake your second pizza.

Note: If making on the same day, start making your dough at least three hours before you plan to eat your pizzas. Freeze remaining quantity of pizza dough to use another time.

Baked chickpea, leek & potato samosas with toasted coconut & coriander chutney

hands-on time	1 hour
total time	1 hour 30 mins
makes	24 samosas

(VE)   (S) (A) (W)

Baking samosas, rather than deep-frying them, means they can all be cooked at once, and are a healthier choice but still have that classic taste and crispness. These are best made with a second pair of hands – what better way to connect.

First make the samosa pastry. In a large bowl, sift together the flours and sea salt. Pour the oil into the flours and using your hands, rub together to form a rough crumb. Toast the cumin and coriander seeds in a frying pan over medium heat for 2 minutes until fragrant. Use a mortar and pestle to roughly crush. Stir the crushed seeds into the flour. Gradually add about 220ml cold water to the flour mixture, mixing and kneading with your hands, adding just enough water to form a firm, rough dough. Shape into a disc and cover the dough with a damp tea towel. Set aside to rest for 30 minutes.

For the samosa filling, place the potatoes in a saucepan and cover with water. Bring to the boil over high heat and cook for 10–15 minutes, until tender (a knife should go through each potato easily). Meanwhile, heat the canola oil in a large frying pan over medium heat. Add the seeds and fry for 2 minutes, until fragrant and starting to pop. Add the leek and sauté for 7 minutes, until softened and starting to turn golden. Add the spring onion, lemon zest, ginger, chilli, garam masala and turmeric. Cook for a further 2 minutes. Drain the potatoes and add to the frying pan. Stir in the chickpeas and cook for 5 minutes, mashing the potatoes and chickpeas a little as you go, but keeping some small chunks for texture. Stir in the coriander, lemon juice, salt and pepper. Transfer to a bowl and leave to cool to room temperature.

Preheat the oven to 180°C fan-forced (or 200°C conventional). Line 2 large oven trays with baking paper.

To assemble the samosas, divide the pastry into 12 even pieces (about 80g each) and roll each piece into a ball. Set a small bowl of water beside you. Take one ball at a time (leaving the rest under the damp tea towel) and on a clean surface roll out into a 15–20cm wide circle. Cut in half. Working with one half at a time, wet the straight edge of the pastry with a little water. Fold the pastry in half, pressing the straight edge lightly to seal and keeping the rounded side open, forming a cone shape. Fill the cone with about 2 heaped tsp of filling. Lightly wet the inside edge of the cone opening and press the edges together to form a slightly curved seam that fully encloses the filling. The samosa should have 3 points, two straight sides, and one slightly curved side. Repeat with the other pastry half and then with the remaining pastry and filling to form 24 samosas. As you make the samosas, cover them with a

Samosa pastry

300g plain flour

300g spelt flour

1 tsp sea salt

125ml canola oil

2 tsp cumin seeds

2 tsp coriander seeds

Samosa filling

600g agria potatoes, peeled and chopped into 3cm chunks

2 tbsp canola oil, plus extra to brush

1 tsp cumin seeds

1 tsp coriander seeds

1 tsp black mustard seeds

1 large leek, white and pale green part only, halved lengthways and cut into 5mm slices

2 spring onions, finely chopped

finely grated zest and freshly squeezed juice of 1 lemon

1 tbsp finely grated fresh ginger

1 red or green bird's-eye chilli, finely chopped

1 tsp garam masala

1 tsp ground turmeric

400g can chickpeas, rinsed and drained

3 tbsp finely chopped coriander

1 ½ tsp sea salt

½ tsp cracked black pepper

Toasted coconut & coriander chutney

35g thread coconut

1 large bunch coriander, leaves picked (25g leaves)

10 mint leaves

1 tbsp finely grated fresh ginger

¾ tsp ground cumin

¼ tsp ground turmeric

freshly squeezed juice of 1 lemon

165ml coconut cream

sea salt, to taste

damp tea towel. Brush each samosa all over with a little canola oil and place onto the oven trays. Bake for 40 minutes, turning the samosas and swapping the trays halfway through, until golden brown.

For the toasted coconut & coriander chutney, toast the coconut in a frying pan over medium heat, until golden brown. Transfer to a blender or food processor, add the remaining ingredients (except salt), and blitz to make a relatively smooth chutney. Season to taste with salt.

Serve the samosas hot with the chutney on the side for dipping.

Note: These samosas can be made in advance and frozen before baking. Freeze on a baking paper-lined tray and once solid, transfer to a plastic container or ziplock bag and freeze for up to 3 months. When ready to eat, thaw, brush with oil, and bake as directed.

hands-on time	15 mins
total time	15 mins
serves	6–8 as a side

Black bean noodle, avocado & mango salad with sesame & miso dressing

I call this **BAM & SAM** noodle salad, an acronym for the key ingredients, and it's perfect for when you need to slap something together at short notice. Black bean noodles are high in fibre and gluten-free; they can be found at most supermarkets but you could use soba noodles instead.

First cook the edamame and noodles. Bring a large saucepan of water to the boil over high heat. Add the edamame beans and cook for 2 minutes. Add the noodles to the pan and cook for a further 3–4 minutes, until the noodles are bite-tender and the edamame are cooked. Drain into a colander, rinse with cold water to cool, drain again and transfer to a large bowl.

In a separate bowl, gently toss together the mango, avocado and spring onion with the lemon juice to coat. Add to the noodles and edamame and set aside. Toast the buckwheat and sesame seeds in a small frying pan over medium-high heat for a couple of minutes, until the white seeds start turning golden. Remove from the heat and transfer to a bowl to cool.

For the sesame & miso dressing, place all the dressing ingredients in a bowl and whisk until well combined.

To assemble, add three-quarters of the chopped mint and three-quarters of the dressing to the salad and toss through to combine. Transfer to a serving platter and drizzle with the remaining dressing. Sprinkle with the remaining mint and toasted buckwheat and seeds. Serve immediately, or refrigerate and serve chilled.

Noodle salad

225g fresh or frozen shelled edamame beans

300g black bean noodles

flesh of 2 ripe mangoes, chopped into 2–3cm chunks

flesh of 2 large avocados, cubed

2 spring onions, finely chopped

freshly squeezed juice of ½ lemon

1 tbsp buckwheat groats

1 tbsp white sesame seeds

1 tbsp black sesame seeds

1 bunch mint, leaves picked and roughly chopped

Sesame & miso dressing

4 tbsp rice wine vinegar

3 tbsp sesame oil

2 tbsp shiro (white) miso paste

2 tbsp mirin

2 tbsp maple syrup

1 tbsp tahini

1 tbsp gluten-free light soy sauce

freshly squeezed juice of 1 lemon

2 cloves garlic, finely grated

1 tbsp finely grated fresh ginger

½ tsp ground chilli

Anatomy of a sharing plate

Sharing plates are one of my favourite ways to eat. I love the layering of different textures and flavours, and often you can make the components in advance. They lend themselves well to group dinners, where two or three plates could be served together, or eaten as a quick throw-together meal. My sharing plate formula consists of three layers: a spreadable dip, sauce or grain for 'The Base', some hearty veg or protein as 'The Body', and a zingy or crunchy finish to give it 'The Lift'. Below are examples of how I've used this formula in a number of recipes, and some ideas to construct your own unique sharing plates.

	Layer 1 – 'The Base'	Layer 2 – 'The Body'	Layer 3 – 'The Lift'
Walnut-sesame halloumi (page 50)	spring onion cannellini purée	capsicum halloumi	honey, chilli, capers chopped herbs
Star anise kūmara (page 93)	cauliflower rice	roasted kūmara	midnight dressing
Cucumbers & tomatoes (page 61)	pomegranate & tahini sauce	cucumbers tomatoes	za'atar olive oil
Roasted aubergines (page 65)	sesame labneh	roasted aubergines cherry tomatoes	tamarind sauce toasted sesame seeds chopped parsley
Roasted brassica & lentil salad (page 71)	orange cream	roasted brassicas lentils	chilli oil roasted almonds
Baba ganoush (page 74)	baba ganoush	roasted figs	roasted walnuts pomegranate & balsamic
Citrus-roasted broccolini (page 81)	hazelnut romesco	roasted broccolini	maple-roasted hazelnuts rocket & mint
Build your own sharing plate	yoghurt or labneh hummus, dip, or purée pesto or tapenade thick sauce cooked rice or grains salad greens cooked pasta	roasted, sautéed, or chopped fresh veg pulses (e.g. chickpeas) fried halloumi or paneer crispy tofu shredded meats	chopped herbs pomegranate seeds fried sage or curry leaves tangy cheese or pickle flavoured oil toasted nuts or seeds punchy dressing spice mix (e.g. dukkah)

Roasted carrot & chickpea salad with grapefruit, mint & ginger dressing

hands-on time	15 mins
total time	35 mins
serves	6–8 as a side

(VE) (GF)   (S) (W)

My formula to use leftover veggies in the fridge for a speedy, delicious meal is: veggies (add spice/oil/sweet/salty, then roast); pulses/grains (boil or roast); dressing (acid/salt/oil/herb/spice); texture (nuts/seeds/fresh herbs). This simple salad recipe puts the humble carrot and chickpea into this formula and punches out something both time-efficient and delicious.

Preheat the oven to 200°C fan-forced (or 220°C conventional). Line a large oven tray with baking paper.

First make the grapefruit, mint & ginger dressing. Place all ingredients in a jar, seal tightly with a lid and shake to combine. Set aside to allow the flavours to infuse.

For the roasted carrots & chickpeas, toast the peppercorns, cumin and coriander seeds in a small frying pan over medium-high heat for 2 minutes, until fragrant. Use a mortar and pestle to grind to a coarse powder. Transfer to a large bowl, add the carrots, chickpeas, olive oil, maple syrup and salt. Toss to coat the carrots evenly. Spread out onto the oven tray in a single layer and roast for 20–25 minutes, until the carrots are cooked through but retain a very subtle bite to them. Transfer to the large bowl from earlier. Pour over three-quarters of the dressing and toss through to coat.

Toast the chopped almonds in a frying pan over medium-high heat for a few minutes, tossing occasionally, until turning golden brown.

To serve, pile the roasted carrot salad onto a serving platter. Drizzle with the remaining dressing and top with the toasted almonds and mint leaves. Serve warm or at room temperature.

Grapefruit, mint & ginger dressing

1 bunch mint, leaves picked and roughly chopped

50ml freshly squeezed grapefruit juice

4 tbsp olive oil

2 cloves garlic, finely grated

2 tsp finely grated ginger

½ tsp ground ginger

½ tbsp maple syrup

¼ tsp sea salt

Roasted carrots & chickpeas

1 tsp black peppercorns

1 tsp cumin seeds

1 tsp coriander seeds

600g carrots (about 4), peeled and cut diagonally into 1cm slices

400g can chickpeas, rinsed and drained

2 tbsp olive oil

1 tbsp maple syrup

½ tsp sea salt

50g almonds, roughly chopped

mint leaves, to serve

hands-on time	15 mins
total time	30 mins
serves	4

(VE) (GF) S S A W

Star anise kūmara with cauliflower rice & midnight dressing

Star anise kūmara

1 tbsp coriander seeds
2 tbsp olive oil
1 tbsp maple syrup (or honey if non-vegan)
1 tbsp black sesame seeds
2 tsp ground star anise
½ tsp ground chipotle chilli
2 tbsp grated fresh ginger
4 cloves garlic, roughly chopped
½ tsp sea salt
½ tsp cracked black pepper
600g orange kūmara (about 2), peeled and cut into 2cm chunks
12 sage leaves

Cauliflower rice

½ large cauliflower, leaves removed
freshly squeezed juice of 1 large lemon
2 tbsp finely chopped sage

Midnight dressing

4 tbsp black tahini
2 tbsp balsamic vinegar
1 tbsp maple syrup (or honey if non-vegan)
freshly squeezed juice of 1 lemon
70g unsweetened natural coconut yoghurt
¼ tsp ground chipotle chilli
¼ tsp sea salt
¼ tsp cracked black pepper

Earthy sage and star anise cut through the sweetness of kūmara, and cauliflower rice adds a subtle crunch. Black tahini in the dressing is striking drizzled over this colourful dish, but if it is not available at your local supermarket, you can swap it for regular tahini.

Preheat the oven to 180°C fan-forced (or 200°C conventional). Line a large oven tray with baking paper.

To make the star anise kūmara, use a mortar and pestle to pound the coriander seeds until roughly crushed. In a large bowl, whisk together the olive oil, honey, crushed coriander seeds, black sesame seeds, star anise, chipotle, ginger, garlic, salt and pepper. Add the kūmara and sage leaves and toss to coat. Transfer to the oven tray and spread into a single layer. Roast for 20 minutes, until just cooked through (a knife should go through easily, but you do not want it to be too soft).

Meanwhile, for the cauliflower rice, remove the main stalk from the cauliflower and chop into large florets that are manageable for grating. Using a box grater, grate the cauliflower florets so that it resembles rice. I like to finely grate half and coarsely grate the rest for some added texture, but take care not to grate your fingers! Transfer to a bowl, add the lemon juice and sage and toss to combine.

To make the midnight dressing, combine all the ingredients in a jar and add 50ml hot water. Seal tightly with a lid and shake vigorously until smooth and well-combined, adding a little more hot water if needed to reach a slightly thickened but pourable consistency. Adjust seasoning to taste.

To serve, place the cauliflower rice in the base of a large serving dish, top with the star anise kūmara, and drizzle over the midnight dressing. Serve warm.

Thrive

Simple, speedy meals

While writing this book, on my cycle route to work I would ride by a large luscious patch of grasses. One morning I saw something extraordinary. From this mass of green, dozens of bright white flowers had appeared, their petals open to the sky. That evening when I cycled past again, the flowers had withdrawn, the plants receded to only their basic green. What had I witnessed?

The rain lily, a petite rush-like perennial with deep evergreen leaves, is a common exotic groundcover plant. While its appearance is unremarkable for much of the year, it curiously bursts into flower en masse following a pouring of late-summer rain. The flowers then close at dusk and only reopen when sunlight strikes. Sure enough, the following morning, as I rode down the path with the sun shining, I saw that the flowers had reopened. And for the coming months, after the rain and when the sun shined, the flowers bloomed. This is the environment that allows them to thrive.

But what does it even mean to thrive? Are you a dormant grass, simply surviving, or are you allowing your best self to bloom?

Thriving is as much an attitude as a feeling to be gained. It is joyful and infectious. It is following dreams, ambition and drive. It is self-love, health and strength to share our best with the world. For humans, what we choose to eat is a primary factor that we can control. Balanced, wholesome and creative food can help us to flourish. Rather than cooking to survive, we should be cooking to thrive.

To thrive, our cooking needs to be practical, nourishing and achievable. Food is just one aspect of our busy lives, and in our work-obsessed society, for much of the week we need simple yet nutritious meals. The recipes in this chapter aim to hit that mark. Most can be made in one hour or less and are the types of meals that will quickly become part of your regular repertoire. We're talking minimal fuss for maximum flavour.

Some of these recipes are warming eats that can easily be made ahead and reheated on-the-go, such as 'The OG' mango & mandarin curry (page 108) or Broad bean & leek dal with miso-maple spring onions (page 101). Others focus on fast, fresh ingredients; food that can be thrown together quickly after a draining day or during a busy evening – think Ramen pho with green beans & aubergine (page 127). Recipes where an inspired mouthful prepared in your own kitchen can feel like a flavour getaway at home.

Delicious food does not have to be a labour of love – a little home-cooked joy in our hectic lives can help us to thrive.

Leek & broccoli chowder with crunchy chickpeas & green goblin oil

hands-on time	30 mins
total time	55 mins
serves	4–5 as a main

(VE) (GF)   S A W

This chowder is a riff on the traditional Welsh leek and potato soup. The crunchy chickpeas and green oil are worth repeating beyond this chowder – the chickpeas as a snack and the green oil as a drizzled flavour lift or for dipping bread.

Preheat the oven to 200°C fan-forced (or 220°C conventional). Line a rimmed oven tray with baking paper.

First make the green goblin oil. Use a mortar and pestle to pound the cardamom pods to extract the seeds. Discard the pods. Grind the seeds and peppercorns until roughly crushed. Place the oil in a small saucepan over medium heat and warm for 5 minutes. Remove from the heat and stir in the crushed seeds and peppercorns, chillies and garlic. Cover with a lid and set aside to allow the flavours to infuse into the oil.

For the crunchy chickpeas, place the chickpeas in a single layer on the oven tray and bake for 20 minutes. Transfer the chickpeas to a bowl. Toss with the oil, sumac, chilli and salt. Return to the tray and bake for a further 15–20 minutes or until crunchy, taking care not to burn – there can be a fine line between crunchy and burnt. Transfer to a bowl and season with a little extra sea salt to taste. Set aside.

For the leek & broccoli chowder, cut the leek in half lengthways, then into 1cm-thick slices. Heat the oil in a large heavy-based saucepan over medium heat. Add the leek and sauté for 7 minutes, until starting to soften. Meanwhile, combine the stock and 500ml water in a separate saucepan and bring to the boil over high heat. Reduce the heat to low and keep warm. Sprinkle the flour over the softened leeks and stir through until combined. Add the warm stock, potatoes, broccoli and garlic. Increase the heat to high and bring to the boil, then reduce the heat to medium and simmer for 20–25 minutes, stirring occasionally, until the potatoes are cooked through (a knife should go through each potato with ease). Stir in the milk and dill and simmer for a further 3 minutes. Remove from the heat.

To finish, using a stick blender (or similar), blitz the chowder until relatively smooth (I like to leave the occasional small chunk of potato for texture). Add the lemon juice, salt and pepper and adjust seasoning to taste. Serve hot, topped with the green goblin oil and crunchy chickpeas.

Green goblin oil

10 green cardamom pods

½ tsp black peppercorns

85ml olive oil

2 jalapeño chillies, finely chopped

2 cloves garlic, finely chopped

Crunchy chickpeas

400g can chickpeas, rinsed, drained and dried on paper towel

1 tbsp canola oil

1 tsp ground sumac

½ tsp ground chilli

½ tsp sea salt

Leek & broccoli chowder

1 large leek, white and pale green part only

2 tbsp olive oil

500ml vegetable stock

2 tbsp flour (gluten-free or plain)

1kg agria potatoes, peeled and cut into 2–3cm chunks

1 head broccoli, cut into medium florets

6 cloves garlic, chopped

250ml milk (almond, oat or cow's)

1 tbsp chopped fresh dill, or 1 tsp dried

freshly squeezed juice of ½ lemon

1 ½ tsp sea salt

1 tsp cracked black pepper

Sweetcorn & kūmara fritters with beetroot borani

hands-on time	50 mins
total time	1 hour 15 mins
serves	4–5

These fritters are crunchy and light, studded with bursts of juicy sweetcorn, and packed with knockout flavour. The fritters are paired with a bold and bright beetroot borani, a yoghurt-based Iranian dip. If fresh sweetcorn is out of season, you can easily use frozen kernels.

Preheat the oven to 180°C fan-forced (or 200°C conventional).

First prepare the beetroot borani. Place the beetroot in a large baking dish in a single layer. Pour in 125ml water and cover the dish with foil. Roast for about 40 minutes, until the beetroot is tender (a knife should easily pierce through the flesh). Drain and leave to cool for 5 minutes. Toast the coriander and mustard seeds in a frying pan over medium heat for 2 minutes, until fragrant and starting to pop. Use a mortar and pestle to grind to a rough powder. Place the ground seeds, roasted beetroot and remaining borani ingredients into a food processor and blitz until smooth. Transfer to a bowl and refrigerate until needed.

For the sweetcorn & kūmara fritters, bring a large saucepan of water to the boil over high heat. Add the corn cobs and cook for 5 minutes. Remove the corn from the water and set aside until cool enough to handle. Hold a cob upright on a chopping board and use a sharp knife to cut off the kernels. Repeat with remaining cobs. You should have about 500g kernels. Place 80g of kernels in a small bowl for later and the remaining kernels in a large bowl. To the large bowl of corn kernels, add the kūmara, chickpea flour, coriander, chillies, ginger, lime zest and juice, turmeric, cumin, salt and pepper. Mix to combine. Add 180ml cold water in two parts, stirring after each addition to form a smooth, relatively thick batter. Set aside for 15 minutes to thicken slightly.

To cook the fritters, heat 2–3cm canola oil in a deep frying pan or Dutch oven (about 25cm) over medium heat to about 175°C. Check with a digital instant read thermometer or drop a blob of batter into the oil. If it sizzles, floats and starts to brown, the oil is ready. Line a large plate with paper towel. Place heaped tablespoons of the batter into the hot oil, in batches of 4–5 at a time. Cook for 2–3 minutes on each side, until golden. Use a slotted spoon to transfer to the paper towel to drain. Repeat until all the batter has been cooked, adjusting the heat as needed to maintain the oil temperature.

Beetroot borani

- 500g beetroot, peeled and cut into 2cm chunks
- 1 tbsp coriander seeds
- 1 tsp black mustard seeds
- 210g yoghurt (coconut or unsweetened natural)
- 2 cloves garlic, finely chopped
- 1 tbsp chopped dill
- finely grated zest and freshly squeezed juice of 1 lemon
- 4 tbsp olive oil
- 1 ½ tbsp tahini
- 1 tbsp maple syrup (or honey if non-vegan)
- 1 tsp sea salt
- ½ tsp ground chilli
- ¼ tsp ground cinnamon

Sweetcorn & kūmara fritters

- 3 large corn cobs, husks and silk removed
- 250g kūmara, peeled and finely grated
- 180g chickpea (besan) flour
- 1 handful coriander leaves, roughly chopped
- 2 green chillies, finely chopped
- 1 tbsp finely grated fresh ginger
- finely grated zest and freshly squeezed juice of 1 lime
- 1 tsp ground turmeric
- 1 tsp ground cumin
- 1 tsp sea salt
- ½ tsp cracked black pepper
- canola oil, for frying

1 tsp ground sumac

lime wedges

coriander leaves

To make charred sumac corn, take the small bowl of corn kernels and add the sumac. Toss to coat. Heat a small frying pan over high heat and once starting to smoke, add the corn kernels and cook for 3–5 minutes, tossing occasionally, until starting to char. Remove from the heat and squeeze over a little lime juice.

Serve the fritters warm, with a generous dollop of beetroot borani (I like to spread this on the plate with the back of a spoon), charred sumac corn, coriander leaves and lime wedges.

hands-on time	50 mins
total time	1 hour 15 mins
serves	4 as a main

Broad bean & leek dal with miso-maple spring onions

Broad bean & leek dal

300g dried green lentils

1 medium-large leek, white and pale green part only

2 tbsp coconut oil

2 brown onions, thinly sliced

1 tbsp finely grated fresh ginger

3 cloves garlic, finely chopped

1 green chilli, finely chopped

2 spring onions, thinly sliced

½ tsp ground cinnamon

½ tsp ground turmeric

½ tsp ground cardamom

250ml vegetable stock

400ml can coconut cream

1 ½ tsp sea salt

200g fresh or frozen podded broad beans

freshly squeezed juice of ½ lemon

Miso-maple spring onions

1 tbsp sesame seeds

2 tbsp coconut oil

2 tsp poppy seeds

1 tsp black mustard seeds

3 spring onions, thinly sliced

1 tbsp finely grated fresh ginger

1 tsp chilli flakes

1 ½ tbsp shiro (white) miso paste

2 tbsp maple syrup

freshly squeezed juice of ½ lemon

coriander leaves, to serve

The visual simplicity of dal disguises a soul-warming dish. This recipe walks far from its Indian roots, with miso, maple syrup and broad beans playing off more typical spices.

For the broad bean & leek dal, rinse the lentils in a sieve under cold running water until the water runs clear. Place in a bowl and cover with cold water until needed. Cut the leek in half lengthways, then into 1cm-thick slices. Heat the coconut oil in a large saucepan over medium heat. Add the leek and onion and sauté for 10 minutes until softened. Add the ginger, garlic, chilli and spring onion and fry for a further 3 minutes, tossing through. Stir in the ground cinnamon, turmeric and cardamom and cook for 1 minute. Drain the lentils and add to the pan with the stock, 200ml of the coconut cream, salt and 650ml water. Stir to combine and bring to the boil over high heat. Reduce the heat to medium-low, cover and simmer for about 40 minutes, stirring occasionally, until the lentils are soft and the dal has reduced and thickened.

Meanwhile, place the broad beans in a bowl, cover with boiling water and leave for 3 minutes. Drain and rinse under cold water. Pop the broad beans out of their husks so you are left with the tender bright green beans. Stir the broad beans, lemon juice and remaining coconut cream into the lentils. Simmer uncovered for a further 3 minutes or until your dal reaches your desired thickness. Remove from the heat and season to taste with extra salt if needed.

For the miso-maple spring onions, toast the sesame seeds in a frying pan over medium heat for a couple of minutes, until starting to turn light golden. Add the coconut oil, poppy and mustard seeds, spring onion, ginger and chilli flakes. Sauté for 5 minutes, until the spring onion is soft. In a bowl, whisk together the miso paste, maple syrup, lemon juice and 65ml warm water. Pour the liquid into the hot pan and cook for a further 3 minutes, stirring through the spring onion until it reduces a little and is starting to caramelise.

Serve the dal warm, topped with the miso-maple spring onions and coriander leaves.

Chilli basil beef with black bean rice

hands-on time	40 mins
total time	1 hour
	(+ marinating time)
serves	3–4 as a main

Soy sauce is an excellent tenderiser here, breaking down some of the proteins in the meat for ultimate succulence. It's deliciously paired with cherry tomatoes, basil, chilli, and a spin on Belizean rice and beans.

To prepare the beef, place the steak in a shallow dish. Mix the soy sauce, oil, vinegar, honey, garlic, basil, chilli, paprika, salt and pepper in a small bowl. Pour the marinade over the beef and massage into the meat, turning to evenly coat. Refrigerate for 1 hour to marinate. Take out 30 minutes before cooking to allow the meat to come to room temperature.

For the black bean rice, heat the oil in a medium-large saucepan over medium heat. Add the onion and capsicum and sauté for 8 minutes, until starting to soften nicely. Add the cumin seeds and garlic, cook for a further 2 minutes, then remove from the heat. Place the rice in a sieve and rinse under cold running water until the water draining from the rice runs clear. Transfer the rice to the saucepan with the vegetables, add the remaining ingredients and stir through to combine. Cover the saucepan with a lid, place over high heat and bring to the boil. Do NOT remove the lid during the cooking process. As soon as the rice is bubbling vigorously, reduce the heat to low and leave to simmer for 14 minutes. Remove from the heat and leave the rice to stand (with the lid still on) for a further 10 minutes. Remove the lid from the saucepan and fluff up the rice with a fork.

Cook the steak when the rice is almost ready. Heat a large frying pan over medium-high heat (or you can cook on the barbecue). Once very hot, take the steak from the marinade (reserve the remaining marinade) and place into the hot pan. Cook for 3–4 minutes on each side for medium-rare. Transfer to a plate, cover with foil and leave to rest for 8 minutes. While the steak rests, return the frying pan (with any remaining juices and crunchy bits) to medium-high heat. Pour the reserved marinade into the pan, along with the stock and cherry tomatoes. Bring to the boil then reduce the heat to medium-low and simmer for 10 minutes, until slightly reduced and the cherry tomatoes are starting to break down but retain some shape. Remove the sauce from the heat.

To serve, use a sharp knife to slice the steak into thin strips. Divide the Black bean rice evenly between bowls and top with the sliced beef, cherry tomato sauce, pickled chillies and torn basil leaves.

Vegan option: Use portobello mushrooms in place of beef, and maple syrup in place of honey.

Chilli basil beef

600g beef rump steak, 2–3cm thick, fat trimmed

4 tbsp gluten-free light soy sauce

2 tbsp olive oil

1 tbsp apple cider vinegar

1 tbsp honey

4 cloves garlic, finely chopped

2 tbsp finely chopped basil leaves

1 red chilli, finely chopped

1 tsp ground paprika

½ tsp sea salt

½ tsp cracked black pepper

125ml vegetable stock

200g cherry tomatoes

pickled chillies (page 218), to serve

Black bean rice

1 tbsp canola oil

½ red onion, finely chopped

1 red capsicum, cored, deseeded and roughly chopped

1 tbsp cumin seeds

2 cloves garlic, finely chopped

200g jasmine rice

400g can black beans, rinsed and drained

40g currants

250ml coconut cream

250ml vegetable stock

2 tbsp chopped basil leaves, plus extra torn leaves, to serve

hands-on time	15 mins

total time 1 hour 30 mins (oven),
45 mins (stovetop)

serves	3–4

Harissa baked beans

2 tbsp canola oil

1 large red onion, thinly sliced

4 cloves garlic, finely chopped

1 tbsp finely grated fresh ginger

2 x 400g cans cannellini or butter beans, rinsed and drained

400g can chopped tomatoes

2 tbsp tomato paste

1 tbsp rose harissa (page 217)

1 tbsp finely chopped sage, plus extra to serve

1 tsp ground turmeric

1 whole star anise

1 tsp soft brown sugar

1 tsp sea salt

yoghurt (coconut or unsweetened natural), to serve

gluten-free bread or yoghurt flatbreads (page 231), warmed to serve

A can of baked beans will always have its place in the pantry, but there's no question that these beans are everything I wish the canned food icon could be. The combination of rose harissa (a floral North African chilli paste), earthy sage, and warming ginger sings through the spiced, and not-too-sweet tomato sauce. If you have the time, bake this in the oven for the best flavour. The stovetop method produces a close second if speed is in need.

Preheat the oven to 180°C fan-forced (or 200°C conventional).

Heat the oil in a medium–large Dutch oven or flameproof casserole dish over medium heat. Add the onion and sauté for 8 minutes, until soft. Add the garlic and ginger and cook for a further 2 minutes. Remove from the heat and stir in the remaining ingredients and 250ml water. Cover and bake for 1 hour 20 minutes, stirring halfway through. The sauce should end up reasonably thick. Adjust seasoning to taste.

Serve the baked beans hot, with a dollop of coconut yoghurt, chopped fresh sage and the warm flatbreads for dipping.

Note: To save time, you could cook the baked beans on the stovetop instead of transferring to the oven. Bring to the boil, then reduce the heat to medium-low and simmer for 30 minutes or until the sauce is nicely thickened.

Chicken & apricot pasanda

hands-on time	20 mins
total time	45 mins
	(+ marinating time)
serves	3–4 as a main

(GF)

The key to this curry is in the tenderising yoghurt and spice marinade. I like incorporating fruits in curries, and here apricots provide a hint of sweet and sour.

Marinate the chicken at least 4 hours in advance. For the marinade, use a mortar to pestle to pound the cardamom pods to extract the seeds. Discard the pods. Toast the coriander seeds, peppercorns and fennel seeds in a small frying pan over medium–high heat for a minute, until fragrant. Add to the cardamom seeds and crush to as fine a powder as possible, then transfer to a large bowl. Add the turmeric and yoghurt and mix to combine, then stir in the chicken to coat. Refrigerate for a minimum of 4 hours, or overnight. Take out of the fridge 1 hour before cooking.

To make the pasanda, place the dried apricots in a heatproof bowl and cover with 250ml boiling water. Set aside to soak for 10 minutes. Heat the oil in a large, deep frying pan over medium heat. Add the onion and sauté for 8 minutes, until soft. Meanwhile, toast the desiccated coconut in a small frying pan over medium–high heat for a few minutes, until golden. Set aside.

Add the garlic, chilli and ginger to the onion and fry for 2 minutes, then stir in the desiccated coconut, ground almonds and tomato paste and cook for a further minute. Stir in the chicken and marinade, and the apricots with the water. Bring to the boil then reduce the heat to medium–low and simmer for 20 minutes, stirring occasionally, until the chicken is cooked through and the sauce has thickened. Stir in the salt and adjust seasoning to taste.

To serve, toast the chopped almonds in a small frying pan over medium–high heat for a couple of minutes, until starting to turn golden. Add the thread coconut and toast for another minute or two until the coconut and almonds are golden brown. Transfer to a bowl. Serve the pasanda hot, topped with the toasted thread coconut and chopped almonds, coriander leaves and your favourite rice.

---

10 green cardamom pods

1 tbsp coriander seeds

1 tsp black peppercorns

1 tsp fennel seeds

1 tsp ground turmeric

280g unsweetened natural yoghurt

800g boneless chicken thighs, skin removed, cut into 3–4cm chunks

100g dried apricots, roughly chopped

2 tbsp canola oil

1 brown onion, thinly sliced

4 tbsp desiccated coconut

3 cloves garlic, finely chopped

1–2 long red chillies, finely chopped

1 tbsp finely grated fresh ginger

30g ground almonds

2 tbsp tomato paste

1 tsp sea salt

40g almonds, roughly chopped

4 tbsp thread coconut

coriander leaves, to serve

steamed rice (page 215), to serve

hands-on time	35 mins
total time	35 mins
serves	4–5 as a main

Spiced lamb flatbreads with triple black hummus & sumac feta whip

Triple black hummus

400g can black beans, rinsed and drained

juice of 1 small lemon

2 tbsp black tahini

6 pitted black olives

2 cloves garlic, finely chopped

1 tsp honey

½ tsp each sea salt and cracked black pepper

Sumac feta whip

100g feta, finely crumbled

4 tbsp unsweetened natural Greek yoghurt

2 tsp ground sumac

Spiced lamb

3 tbsp canola oil

2 brown onions, finely chopped

4 cloves garlic, finely chopped

1 tbsp finely grated fresh ginger

2 tsp each coriander seeds and cumin seeds

500g lamb mince

1 tsp each ground sumac, dried mint, and dried sage

¼ tsp ground chilli

½ tsp each sea salt and cracked black pepper

1 tbsp pomegranate molasses

1 large handful flat-leaf parsley leaves, finely chopped

To serve

75g hazelnuts, roughly chopped

warm flatbreads (page 231)

chopped flat-leaf parsley leaves

pomegranate molasses, extra

These flatbreads are deeply rooted in flavours of the Middle East and Mediterranean. 'Triple black' comes from the triple threat of black beans, black tahini, and black olives, which are blitzed together to form a delicious dip. Paired with whipped feta and lamb, simple components come together for something sensational.

First make the triple black hummus. Place all ingredients in a food processor or blender and blitz until smooth. Loosen with a little cold water if desired, adjust seasoning to taste and set aside.

For the sumac feta whip, use a fork to mash the feta in a small bowl to form a smooth-ish paste. Stir in the yoghurt and sumac and whisk with a fork until whipped.

For the spiced lamb, heat 2 tbsp oil in a large frying pan over medium heat. Add the onions and sauté for 5 minutes, until starting to soften. Add the garlic and ginger and fry for a further 2 minutes. Use a mortar and pestle to roughly crush the coriander and cumin seeds. Add the crushed seeds, lamb mince, sumac, mint, sage, chilli, salt and pepper to the pan with the remaining oil. Cook for 5 minutes, stirring occasionally, until lightly browned. Add 85ml warm water and simmer for 5 minutes, until the water has evaporated. Stir in the pomegranate molasses and parsley, adjust seasoning to taste, and remove from the heat.

To serve, toast the chopped hazelnuts in a small frying pan over medium heat for 5 minutes, stirring occasionally, until golden brown and fragrant. Remove from the heat and if desired, rub the hazelnuts in a tea towel to remove the skins. Spread some of the triple black hummus over the warm flatbreads. Top with the spiced lamb, a dollop of sumac feta whip, a sprinkle of toasted hazelnuts, a drizzle of pomegranate molasses and extra chopped fresh parsley.

'The OG' mango & mandarin curry

hands-on time	35 mins
total time	1 hour
serves	4 as a main

(VE) (GF)

This curry has been a regular fixture in my kitchen for years, and is rightfully referred to as 'the OG'. The flavours may sound curious – roasted peanuts, tamarind, mango, mandarin – but it's yet to disappoint. Serve with lemon & coriander rice (page 215).

Preheat the oven to 160°C fan-forced (or 180°C conventional). Line an oven tray with baking paper.

First roast the peanuts for the curry paste. Place the peanuts in a single layer on the oven tray and roast for 15 minutes until golden brown. Cool for 5 minutes, then rub with a tea towel to remove any skins.

To make the curry paste, using a stick blender or similar, blitz together the roasted peanuts and remaining paste ingredients. Add a little water if needed, to make a reasonably smooth paste.

For the curry, heat the oil in a large, deep frying pan over medium heat. Add the onion and sauté for 8 minutes, stirring occasionally, until soft. Add the curry paste and cook for a further 2 minutes, stirring through the onions until starting to brown. Add the cauliflower, capsicum, mango and mandarin segments, and heat through for 2 minutes. Stir in the coconut cream and 125ml water then add the salt and pepper. Increase the heat to medium–high and bring to the boil, then reduce the heat to medium and simmer for 15 minutes, stirring occasionally, until the cauliflower is tender and the curry is starting to thicken. Add the beans and coriander and simmer for 3 minutes, until the beans are tender-crisp.

Serve the curry with lemon & coriander rice, a dollop of yoghurt, extra chopped coriander and a sprinkling of fresh pomegranate seeds.

Curry paste

75g raw peanuts

8 cloves garlic, finely chopped

2 long red chillies, chopped

1 thumb-sized piece of ginger, finely chopped

finely grated zest and freshly squeezed juice of 1 lemon

1 tbsp tamarind paste

2 tsp ground turmeric

1 tsp garam masala

½ tsp sea salt

Additional ingredients

2 tbsp canola oil

1 large brown onion, finely chopped

1 cauliflower, cut into medium florets (about 500g)

1 large capsicum, cored, deseeded and thinly sliced

flesh of 1 large mango, roughly chopped

4 mandarins, segmented

400ml can coconut cream

½ tsp sea salt

1 tsp cracked black pepper

150g green beans, ends trimmed, chopped into 5cm pieces

2 tbsp finely chopped coriander

To serve

lemon & coriander rice (page 215)

yoghurt (coconut or unsweetened natural)

chopped coriander, extra

pomegranate seeds

hands-on time	35 mins
total time	35 mins
serves	3–4 as a main

Caramelised leek & mushroom spaghetti with pecan pangrattato

2 large leeks, white and pale green part only

2 tbsp olive oil

½ tsp + 1 tbsp sea salt, plus extra to taste

6 cloves garlic, finely chopped

250g white button mushrooms, sliced

125ml white wine

125ml vegetable stock

1 tbsp fresh or 1 tsp dried thyme

500g spaghetti

freshly squeezed juice of 1 lemon

½ tsp cracked black pepper

Pecan pangrattato

2 tbsp olive oil

50g breadcrumbs

50g pecans, finely chopped

2 cloves garlic, finely chopped

finely grated zest of 1 lemon

2 tbsp finely chopped parsley

large pinch of ground nutmeg

¼ tsp sea salt

¼ tsp cracked black pepper

Giving the leeks time to slowly sauté at the start allows them to caramelise and bring a depth of flavour. I often make a double batch of the pecan pangrattato to have on hand – it provides a crunchy counterpoint perfect for sprinkling over quick pasta dishes, like this spaghetti.

For the pecan pangrattato, heat the olive oil in a frying pan over medium heat. Add the breadcrumbs, chopped pecans and garlic and fry for 3–4 minutes, until golden brown. Remove from the heat and stir through the lemon zest, parsley, nutmeg, salt and pepper.

To make the sauce, cut the leeks in half lengthways, then into 1cm-thick slices. Heat the olive oil in a large frying pan over medium heat. Add the leeks and ½ tsp salt and sauté for 15 minutes, until soft and starting to caramelise. Add the garlic and mushrooms, sauté for a further 3 minutes, then pour in the white wine and stock. Increase the heat to high to bring to the boil, then reduce to medium, add the thyme and simmer for 10–15 minutes, until most of the liquid has evaporated.

Meanwhile, for the spaghetti, bring a large saucepan of water with the remaining 1 tbsp salt to the boil over high heat. Add the spaghetti and cook for 8–10 minutes or as per packet instructions, until al dente. Drain, reserving 60ml of the cooking water. Add the spaghetti and water to the frying pan with the leeks and mushrooms. Remove from the heat and add the lemon juice and pepper. Toss through the spaghetti and season with a little extra salt to taste, if desired.

Serve the spaghetti warm, topped with a generous sprinkling of pecan pangrattato.

Tricolour kofta with special curry sauce

hands-on time	40 mins
total time	1 hour
serves	4 as a main

It's fun to cook with colour. Here I use zucchini, parsnip and carrot, but you could use grated pumpkin or beetroot instead. The kofta are delicate, so add them to the sauce only when serving.

Preheat the oven to 180°C fan-forced (or 200°C conventional). Line an oven tray with baking paper.

First, prepare the vegetables for the tricolour kofta. Place the zucchini, carrot and parsnip in a large sieve over a bowl. Sprinkle with the salt and use your hands to mix through. Leave for 20 minutes, to allow the salt to draw the water out of the vegetables.

Meanwhile, for the special curry sauce, heat the oil in a large frying pan over medium heat. Once hot, add the sliced onion and sauté for 8 minutes until soft. Stir in the garlic and ginger and cook for 2 minutes, until starting to turn golden. Stir in the spices and curry leaves, cooking for 30 seconds. Pour in the orange juice, simmer for 1 minute, then stir in the stock, tomatoes, salt and pepper. Increase the heat to medium–high, sprinkle over the ground almonds and stir through. Bring to the boil then reduce the heat to medium and leave to simmer for 15 minutes, stirring occasionally, until the sauce has reduced and thickened. Pour in the coconut cream, stir through, then reduce the heat to low and simmer for a further 5 minutes. Remove from the heat and adjust seasoning to taste.

To make the kofta, take a handful of the grated vegetables at a time, squeeze out as much liquid as possible, and transfer to a large bowl. You should have around 450g of grated vegetables. Add the remaining kofta ingredients (except the oil and yoghurt) and mix together with your hands, squeezing the vegetables as you go, to form a rollable consistency. Roll the mixture into 12 golf ball-sized balls and place onto the oven tray. Drizzle with a little canola oil and bake for 25 minutes, until golden brown and crispy.

To serve, reheat the curry sauce over medium heat. Serve the kofta in bowls with the curry sauce, yoghurt, extra herbs and coconut rice or flatbreads.

Tricolour kofta

300g zucchinis (about 2), coarsely grated

300g carrots (about 2), peeled and coarsely grated

200g parsnips (about 1 large), peeled and coarsely grated

1 ½ tsp sea salt

finely grated zest of 1 orange

2 cloves garlic, finely grated

1 tsp ground cumin

1 tsp ground coriander

1 tsp garam masala

½ tsp cracked black pepper

2 tbsp finely chopped flat-leaf parsley leaves, plus extra to serve

2 tbsp finely chopped mint leaves, plus extra to serve

60g fine breadcrumbs

25g chickpea (besan) flour

canola oil, for drizzling

yoghurt (coconut or unsweetened natural), to serve

Special curry sauce

2 tbsp canola oil

1 large brown onion, thinly sliced

4 cloves garlic, finely chopped

1 tbsp finely grated fresh ginger

1 tsp ground cumin

1 tsp ground coriander

1 tsp ground turmeric

1 tsp garam masala

¾ tsp ground chilli

½ tsp ground cinnamon

12 curry leaves

60ml freshly squeezed orange juice

250ml vegetable stock

400g can chopped tomatoes

¾ tsp sea salt

½ tsp cracked black pepper

3 tbsp ground almonds

125ml coconut cream

To serve

coconut rice (page 215) or flatbreads (page 231)

hands-on time	30 mins
total time	45 mins
serves	4 as a main

(GF)

Monkfish laksa with Thai basil & curry leaves

Laksa paste

75g cashews

4 kaffir lime leaves, shredded

4 cloves garlic, finely chopped

3 shallots, finely chopped

2 stalks lemongrass, tough outer layers removed, ends trimmed and chopped

2 red chillies, finely chopped

3 tbsp chopped Thai basil

2 tbsp fish sauce

1 tbsp finely grated fresh ginger

1 tbsp caster sugar

1 tbsp tamarind paste

1 tsp each ground coriander and ground turmeric

½ tsp cracked black pepper

finely grated zest and freshly squeezed juice of 1 lime

Additional ingredients

3 tbsp coconut oil

1 litre vegetable stock

400ml can coconut cream

2 tbsp fish sauce

20 curry leaves

500g monkfish fillets (or any firm white-fleshed fish), chopped into 3cm chunks

250g green beans, ends trimmed and halved

1 tbsp soft brown sugar

1 tsp sea salt

1 large handful Thai basil leaves, roughly chopped, plus extra to serve

200g rice vermicelli noodles

mung bean sprouts, to serve

Tamarind, lemongrass and kaffir lime form the basis for this slurpingly good noodle soup. It hits you first with the aromas of citrus, Thai basil and curry. Then comes the coconut broth, rich with fish sauce umami, warming chilli and ginger.

First make the laksa paste. Toast the cashews in a frying pan over medium heat for a few minutes, tossing occasionally, until golden brown. Roughly chop half the cashews and set aside. Transfer the other half of the cashews and remaining laksa paste ingredients to a blender or food processor and blitz to form a relatively smooth paste.

To cook the laksa, heat the coconut oil in a medium-large saucepan over medium heat. Add the laksa paste and fry for 5 minutes, until deeply fragrant and starting to brown. Stir in the stock, coconut cream, fish sauce and curry leaves. Increase heat to high to bring to the boil, then reduce to medium and simmer for 15 minutes. Add the monkfish, green beans, brown sugar and salt. Increase the heat to medium–high and simmer for a further 4 minutes, until the fish is just cooked through and the beans are tender-crisp. Remove from the heat, stir through the lime juice and basil and adjust seasoning to taste.

As the laksa is simmering, prepare the noodles. Place the vermicelli noodles in a large heatproof bowl, pour over boiling water to cover and leave to soften for 5 minutes. Drain, refresh under cold water, and drain again.

To serve, divide the noodles evenly among four bowls. Ladle over the laksa and top with a handful of mung bean sprouts, the reserved cashews, and extra basil.

Pumpkin, persimmon & ginger soup with Cajun seeds

hands-on time	25 mins
total time	50 mins
serves	6 as a main

(VE) (GF) (A) (W)

You'll be hard pressed to find a bowl of soup that catches the essence of late autumn quite like this one. If persimmons are hard to come by, carrots are a fair substitute.

Preheat the oven to 160°C fan-forced (or 180°C conventional). Line an oven tray with baking paper.

For the Cajun seeds, toss all the ingredients together in a bowl to coat the seeds evenly. Spread the mixture out in a single layer on the oven tray. Roast for 15 minutes, until crunchy and starting to turn golden brown. Remove from the oven and set aside to cool.

For the soup, heat the olive oil in a large heavy-based saucepan over medium heat. Add the onion and sauté for 10 minutes, until soft and starting to caramelise a little. Add the garlic, ginger, chilli, cumin, turmeric and cinnamon. Toss through the onion for a minute, until the spices are starting to brown, then add the pumpkin and persimmon and mix through. Pour in the vegetable stock and 250ml water, increase the heat to high and bring to the boil. Once the soup is bubbling vigorously, reduce the heat to medium and simmer for 15 minutes, until the pumpkin is tender. Remove from the heat and using a stick blender (or similar), blitz the soup until smooth. Stir in the coconut cream, coriander leaves and pepper. The soup will be a bit thin at this point, so return to medium heat and simmer until reduced to your desired consistency. Remove from the heat and blitz once more with the stick blender to smooth out any remaining lumps. Stir in the lemon juice and season with salt to taste (I find around 2 tsp is usually about right for me).

To serve, ladle the warm soup into bowls and drizzle with a little yoghurt. Top with the Cajun seeds and a few coriander leaves.

3 tbsp olive oil

2 brown onions, thinly sliced

6 cloves garlic, finely chopped

2 tbsp finely grated ginger

1 long red chilli, finely chopped

1 tbsp ground cumin

2 tsp ground turmeric

1 tsp ground cinnamon

1 kg peeled butternut pumpkin flesh (from 1 butternut), chopped into 2cm chunks

500g Fuyu persimmons (about 3), ends removed, chopped into 1cm chunks

625ml vegetable stock

400ml can coconut cream

1 large handful coriander leaves, plus extra to serve

1 tsp cracked black pepper

freshly squeezed juice of ½ lemon

sea salt, to taste

yoghurt (coconut or unsweetened natural), to serve

Cajun seeds

75g pumpkin seeds

2 tbsp olive oil

finely grated zest of ½ lemon

1 tsp ground paprika

½ tsp garlic powder

½ tsp cracked black pepper

½ tsp ground cayenne pepper

½ tsp dried oregano

½ tsp sea salt

hands-on time	25 mins
total time	50 mins
serves	2 as a main

Preserved lemon teriyaki salmon with spring greens & soba

Marinated salmon

4 tbsp light soy sauce

2 tbsp mirin

1 tbsp honey

1 tbsp sesame oil

1 tbsp rice wine vinegar

2 cloves garlic, finely grated

1 tbsp finely grated fresh ginger

skin of ½ preserved lemon, finely chopped

½ green chilli, finely chopped

2 x 150–200g salmon fillets, skin on, bones removed

Additional ingredients

160g green tea soba noodles

75g fresh or frozen shelled edamame beans

120g green beans, ends trimmed and halved

2 spring onions, finely chopped

1 small bunch (10g) coriander, leaves picked, plus extra to serve

freshly squeezed juice of 1 lemon

2 tbsp olive oil

1 tbsp black sesame seeds

1 tbsp white sesame seeds

Preserved lemons can be found at specialty food stores and some supermarkets, but it's easy to make them (page 218). After bathing the salmon, I pan-fry it for a crispier skin, but it can be wrapped in foil and baked if desired.

First marinate the salmon. In a bowl, whisk together the soy sauce, mirin, honey, sesame oil, vinegar, garlic, ginger, preserved lemon and chilli. Pat the salmon fillets dry with paper towel, place in a dish and pour over the marinade. Cover and refrigerate for 30 minutes.

For the greens & soba, bring a medium–large saucepan of water to the boil over medium-high heat. Add the noodles and edamame beans and cook for 2 minutes, then add the green beans and cook for a further 2–3 minutes until the noodles are just tender and the beans are tender-crisp. Drain, rinse with cold water to cool, drain again and transfer to a large bowl. Toss through the spring onion, coriander leaves and lemon juice.

To cook the salmon, heat the olive oil in a large frying pan over medium-high heat. Add the salmon skin-side down, reserving the marinade. Reduce the heat to medium and cook the salmon, pressing with a spatula to stop them from curling, for 3 minutes, until the skin is crispy. Turn and cook for a further 2–3 minutes, until almost cooked through. Remove from the pan and set aside, skin-side up. Pour the reserved marinade into the hot frying pan and simmer over medium heat for 2 minutes to reduce a little and caramelise, then remove from the heat.

To serve, in a small frying pan over medium heat, toast the sesame seeds for a few minutes until golden brown. Transfer to a bowl to cool. Add three-quarters of the cooked marinade and half the sesame seeds to the noodles, tossing to coat. Arrange the dressed noodles in bowls, place the salmon fillets on top (skin side up), brush with the remaining marinade, and sprinkle with the remaining sesame seeds and extra coriander.

Sumac yoghurt chicken with orange tabbouleh & green olive hummus

hands-on time	30 mins
total time	50 mins
	(+ overnight marinate)
serves	4 as a main

This combines elements that are excellent together but versatile on their own. Oranges bring a jewel-like quality to the tabbouleh and lends it some sweetness.

Marinate the sumac yoghurt chicken in advance. Place all the ingredients, except the chicken, in a large bowl and mix to combine. Add the chicken and toss through the marinade to coat. Refrigerate for at least 3 hours (or overnight). Remove the chicken from the fridge 30 minutes before cooking.

Preheat the oven to 170°C fan-forced (or 190°C conventional). Line a large roasting dish with baking paper. Transfer the chicken and marinade to the roasting dish and bake for 35 minutes, until the chicken is cooked through.

While the chicken is cooking, make the orange tabbouleh. If using fine bulgur, place in a fine sieve and rinse under cold water several times until the water runs reasonably clear. Drain, transfer to a bowl and fluff up with a fork. If using medium bulgur, place in a bowl, cover with boiling water and soak for 10–15 minutes until tender but still firm to the bite. Drain and fluff up with a fork. Finely chop the parsley and mint leaves and add to the bulgur wheat, along with the spring onion, shallot, lemon zest and juice, olive oil, salt and pepper. Finely grate the zest of one orange and add to the tabbouleh. Cut the skin and white pith off the oranges, then cut out the segments, discarding the inner pith and membranes. Toss the segments through the tabbouleh and set aside.

For the green olive hummus, place all the ingredients and 4 tbsp cold water in a food processor or blender and blitz until smooth.

To finish the chicken, turn the oven to the grill function and grill the chicken for 5–10 minutes, until starting to brown a little on top. Set aside for 5 minutes then transfer the chicken to a chopping board and cut into slices.

To serve, toast the pine nuts in a small frying pan over medium heat, until golden brown. Serve the chicken warm with the orange tabbouleh, green olive hummus, toasted pine nuts and some extra chopped parsley.

Sumac yoghurt chicken

280g unsweetened natural yoghurt

4 tbsp olive oil

1 tbsp finely chopped fresh oregano

1 tbsp ground sumac

½ tsp ground cinnamon

½ tsp ground allspice

½ tsp ground chilli

½ tsp cracked black pepper

1 tsp sea salt

2 cloves garlic, finely chopped

finely grated zest and freshly squeezed juice of 1 lemon

1kg boneless chicken thigh fillets, fat trimmed

Orange tabbouleh

100g fine or medium bulgur wheat

1 extra-large bunch (100g) flat-leaf parsley, leaves picked, plus extra to serve

20g mint leaves

1 spring onion, finely chopped

1 shallot, finely chopped

finely grated zest and freshly squeezed juice of 1 lemon

85ml olive oil

½ tsp sea salt

½ tsp cracked black pepper

2 large oranges

Green olive hummus

400g can chickpeas, rinsed and drained

freshly squeezed juice of ½ lemon

12 green pitted olives

2 cloves garlic, finely chopped

4 tbsp olive oil

2 tbsp tahini

1 tbsp finely chopped flat-leaf parsley

1 tsp honey

½ tsp sea salt

½ tsp cracked black pepper

Additional ingredients

2 tbsp pine nuts

1 large handful flat-leaf parsley leaves, roughly chopped

hands-on time	30 mins
total time	1 hour
serves	4 as a main

Drunken meatballs

Meatballs

500g pork mince

40g fine breadcrumbs

4 cloves garlic, finely chopped

1 handful flat-leaf parsley leaves, finely chopped

1 egg

½ brown onion, finely chopped

2 tbsp tomato paste

2 tbsp finely grated parmesan

2 tsp ground paprika

½ tsp each sea salt and cracked black pepper

3 tbsp olive oil

50g plain flour, for coating

Drunken sauce

250ml red wine

400g can chopped tomatoes

250ml vegetable stock

3 cloves garlic, finely chopped

4 tbsp tomato paste

2 tbsp balsamic vinegar

1 tbsp soft brown sugar

1 tbsp finely chopped fresh basil, or 1 tsp dried

½ tsp each ground chilli and cracked black pepper

¾ tsp sea salt

To serve

500g spaghetti

grated parmesan

finely chopped flat-leaf parsley

fresh basil leaves

The palate of this recipe is classic, but with subtle flavour boosts – parmesan in the meatballs, chilli in the sauce. Pork mince gives the meatballs a lightness, but you could use beef or lamb. A hefty glass of red wine is thrown in for good measure; drunken by name, intoxicatingly tasty.

To prepare the meatballs, use your hands to mix the meatball ingredients (except the olive oil and flour) in a large bowl until well combined. Shape the mixture into 16 golf ball-sized balls and refrigerate for 10 minutes.

Heat the olive oil in a large, deep frying pan over medium-high heat. Place the flour on a plate and roll each meatball in the flour until lightly coated. Place the meatballs into the frying pan. Cook, turning with tongs occasionally, for about 10 minutes, until evenly browned all over. Transfer to a plate and set aside.

For the drunken sauce, return the frying pan to medium-high heat. Add a splash of wine to deglaze the pan then add the remaining red wine, along with the rest of the drunken sauce ingredients (except the salt and pepper). Bring to the boil then reduce the heat to medium. Add the meatballs and coat with the sauce. Simmer for 25–30 minutes, turning the meatballs occasionally to prevent sticking, until the sauce is nicely thickened and the meatballs are cooked through. Stir in the salt and pepper and adjust to taste.

For the spaghetti, while the meatballs are cooking, bring a large saucepan of water with 1 tbsp salt to the boil over high heat. Add the spaghetti and cook for 8–10 minutes or as per packet instructions, until al dente. Drain.

To serve, toss half the drunken sauce through the spaghetti then divide among serving bowls. Top with the meatballs and remaining sauce, and sprinkle with parmesan, parsley and basil.

Massaman potato frittata

hands-on time	40 mins
total time	1 hour
serves	4–6 as a main

(GF) S S A W

The key to massaman's success is in its aromatic paste, but why confine it to curry? The paste can be made in advance and refrigerated until needed. Serve with tomato, date & tamarind chutney (page 220).

Preheat the oven to 160°C fan-forced (or 180°C conventional).

First make the massaman paste. Use a mortar and pestle to bash open the cardamom pods to release the seeds, discarding the pods. Toast the cardamom seeds, coriander seeds, cumin seeds, peppercorns and cloves in a frying pan over medium heat for a minute or two, until fragrant. Use the mortar and pestle to grind to a fine powder. Using a stick blender or food processor, blitz together the ground spices and remaining paste ingredients, adding a little water if needed, to make a relatively smooth paste.

For the frittata, place the potatoes in a saucepan, cover with cold water and add 1 tsp of sea salt. Bring to the boil over high heat. Cook for about 10 minutes, until just tender. Drain, return to the saucepan and set aside. Heat a large cast iron or ovenproof frying pan (26–28cm) over medium heat. Add the coconut oil and once melted, add the onion and sauté for 8 minutes, until nicely softened. Add 4 tbsp of the massaman paste and 2 tbsp of the coconut cream and cook for 2 minutes, stirring through the onion to brown slightly. Tip the onion mixture onto the potatoes and toss through. In a large bowl, whisk the eggs, remaining coconut cream, coriander, pepper and remaining ½ tsp salt until just combined. Add the potato mixture to the egg mixture and stir to combine.

Wipe out the base of the frying pan with paper towel. Add the olive oil and place over medium heat, tilting the pan to coat it evenly. Once hot, pour the frittata mixture into the centre of the pan, shaking to distribute the mixture evenly. Cook for 5 minutes, until the frittata starts to set at the bottom and sides but the top is still liquid. Crumble over the feta, place pan into the oven and bake for about 20 minutes, until golden brown and set. Remove from the oven and leave to cool a little before serving warm, with a generous dollop of chutney, a sprinkling of peanuts, and salad greens.

Massaman paste

8 green cardamom pods

2 tsp coriander seeds

2 tsp cumin seeds

1 tsp black peppercorns

4 whole cloves

40g roasted peanuts

6 cloves garlic, finely chopped

2 red chillies, finely chopped

2 shallots, finely chopped

1 stalk lemongrass, tough outer layers removed, end trimmed, very thinly sliced

1 tbsp finely grated fresh ginger

1 tbsp tamarind paste

1 tsp each ground cinnamon, soft brown sugar and sea salt

Frittata

500g agria potatoes, peeled and chopped into 2cm chunks

1 ½ tsp sea salt

1 tbsp coconut oil

1 red onion, finely chopped

160ml coconut cream

8 eggs, lightly beaten

2 tbsp finely chopped fresh coriander leaves

½ tsp cracked black pepper

3 tbsp olive oil

75g feta

To serve

tomato, date & tamarind chutney (page 220)

chopped roasted peanuts

salad leaves

hands-on time	30 mins
total time	40 mins
serves	4 as a main

Ramen pho with green beans & aubergine

Spiced aubergine

1 large aubergine (about 400g), chopped into 2–3cm chunks

1 tsp ground cumin

¾ tsp sea salt

½ tsp ground turmeric

½ tsp ground star anise

½ tsp ground ginger

finely grated zest of 1 lemon

freshly squeezed juice of ½ lemon

75ml canola oil

Pho

3 tbsp canola oil

8 cloves garlic, thinly sliced

1 thumb-sized piece of ginger, peeled and thinly sliced

2 stalks lemongrass, tough outer layers removed

2 whole star anise

1–2 red chillies, sliced

500ml vegetable stock

6 tbsp fish sauce

2 tbsp apple cider vinegar

2 tbsp soft brown sugar

freshly squeezed juice of ½ lemon

1 tsp sea salt

400g ramen noodles

250g green beans, ends trimmed

2 spring onions, chopped

coriander leaves, to serve

Vietnamese mint leaves, to serve

Typically, pho is made from a broth of beef or chicken bones. This is my 30-minute vegetarian (and easily veganised) version. I prefer ramen noodles, but vermicelli or flat rice noodles will also do well.

First make the spiced aubergine. Place all the ingredients (except 1 tbsp of oil) in a large bowl and toss to coat the aubergine evenly. Set aside for 5 minutes, to allow the aubergine to soak up most of the oil. Heat the remaining 1 tbsp oil in a large frying pan over medium-high heat. Add the aubergine and cook for 8 minutes, tossing occasionally, until starting to soften. Add 165ml cold water, reduce the heat to medium and cover with a lid. Simmer for 5–6 minutes, until the aubergine is cooked through and most of the water has been cooked off. Remove from the heat.

To prepare the pho, heat the canola oil in a large saucepan over medium heat. Add the garlic, ginger, lemongrass, star anise and chillies. Fry for 2 minutes, until the garlic is starting to turn light golden in colour. Add the stock, fish sauce, vinegar, sugar, lemon juice, salt and 750ml water. Bring to the boil, then reduce the heat to medium-low and simmer gently for 10 minutes, to allow the flavours to infuse.

When almost ready to serve, bring a large saucepan of water to the boil over high heat. Add the ramen noodles and cook for 3 minutes. Add the green beans and cook for a further 2 minutes, until the beans are tender-crisp and the ramen noodles are tender. Drain, rinse with cold water to cool, and drain again.

To serve, use tongs to divide the ramen noodles and beans among four bowls. Strain the hot pho through a sieve and pour over the noodles. Top with the warm aubergine, chopped spring onion and a hefty amount of coriander and Vietnamese mint leaves.

Vegan option: Use vegan fish sauce or light soy sauce in place of regular fish sauce.

Sweet & sour tofu with creamy coconut polenta

hands-on time	40 mins
total time	40 mins (+ marinating)
serves	4 as a main

It's that 'sweet & sour' combo we all love, but without the usual sugary tomato sauce. The tofu is marinated, coated in cornflour for crispiness when shallow-fried, and served on creamy plant-based polenta to soak up all the saucy deliciousness.

For the sweet & sour tofu, whisk the soy sauce, maple syrup, vinegars, sesame oil, ground spices, garlic and ginger in a bowl. Pat the tofu chunks dry with paper towel and place in the marinade, tossing gently to coat. Refrigerate for a minimum of 1 hour (or overnight).

Remove the tofu from the bowl and reserve the marinade. Pat each side of the tofu with paper towel to absorb some of the excess marinade. Heat the oil in a large frying pan over medium–high heat. Place the cornflour in a shallow dish, coat each piece of tofu in the cornflour and shallow-fry in the hot oil for about 4 minutes each side, until crispy and golden brown. Remove the tofu from the pan and place on a paper towel-lined plate to drain any excess oil.

In the same frying pan over medium–high heat, add the red onion and cabbage and sauté for 5 minutes, until starting to soften. Add the capsicum and pineapple and cook for a further 5 minutes, until the pineapple is starting to caramelise. Pour over the reserved marinade, reduce the heat to medium-low and simmer for a further 3 minutes. Remove from the heat.

To make the creamy coconut polenta, place the stock, coconut cream, polenta and salt into a medium–large saucepan over medium heat. Whisking continuously, cook the polenta for 5–10 minutes, until smooth, creamy and thickened (if at any point the polenta is bubbling and spitting at you from the pan, reduce the heat). Remove from the heat and stir through the sesame oil.

To serve, spoon the creamy coconut polenta onto plates and flatten into a large disc with the back of a spoon. Top with the sweet & sour vegetables, crispy tofu and fresh Vietnamese mint leaves.

Sweet & sour tofu

4 tbsp gluten-free light soy sauce

2 tbsp maple syrup

2 tbsp rice wine vinegar

1 tbsp balsamic vinegar

1 tbsp sesame oil

1 tsp ground chilli

1 tsp ground Chinese five spice

½ tsp ground ginger

4 cloves garlic, finely chopped

1 tbsp finely grated fresh ginger

400g firm tofu, drained and cut into 3cm chunks

3 tbsp canola oil

50g cornflour

1 red onion, thinly sliced

¼ medium red cabbage, shredded

1 large red capsicum, cored, deseeded and sliced

250g chopped fresh pineapple, cut into 2–3cm chunks

Vietnamese mint leaves, to serve

Creamy coconut polenta

500ml vegetable stock

400ml can coconut cream

180g instant polenta

1 tsp sea salt

1 tbsp sesame oil

hands-on time	25 mins
total time	40 mins
serves	3–4 as a main

Green coconut broth with shredded chicken & hokkien

Green broth paste

300g frozen peas

10 black peppercorns

1 tsp black mustard seeds

1 tsp fennel seeds

1 tsp coriander seeds

8 cloves garlic, chopped

1 thumb-sized piece of ginger, peeled and finely chopped

2 long green chillies, chopped

1 stalk lemongrass, tough outer layer removed, end trimmed and finely chopped

freshly squeezed juice of 1 lemon

½ tsp sea salt

Additional ingredients

750ml vegetable stock

400ml can coconut cream

3 tbsp fish sauce

1 tbsp caster sugar

1 large handful Vietnamese mint leaves, plus extra to serve (see note)

600g chicken breast fillets

¾ tsp sea salt

400g hokkien noodles

2 heads Shanghai pak choi, ends trimmed, stalks sliced, leaves left whole

A fridge–freezer–pantry raid on a busy weeknight, with wilting veg, almost freezer-burned peas, forgotten noodles plus some pantry staples – we have a winner.

First make the green broth paste. Place the peas in a heatproof bowl and cover with boiling water. Leave for 5 minutes then drain. Toast the peppercorns, mustard, fennel and coriander seeds in a frying pan over medium-high heat for 1–2 minutes until fragrant. Use a mortar and pestle to grind to a rough powder. Place the drained peas, ground spices, garlic, ginger, chillies, lemongrass, lemon juice and salt in a food processor or blender and blitz to a relatively smooth paste.

To cook the broth, combine the green broth paste, stock, coconut cream, fish sauce, sugar, mint, chicken and salt in a large saucepan. Bring to the boil over high heat, then reduce the heat to medium and simmer for about 20 minutes, until the chicken is cooked through. To check, take one breast from the broth and use a small sharp knife to slice two-thirds of the way through the thickest part – the meat should be white the whole way through. Remove the chicken from the broth and place onto a chopping board. Slice the meat, then use two forks to tear into shreds.

Add the noodles and pak choi leaves and stalks to the broth. Simmer for a further 3 minutes, until the noodles are just cooked and the pak choi is tender. Remove from the heat and stir the shredded chicken through the broth. Taste and adjust seasoning as desired. Serve the hot broth topped with extra fresh Vietnamese mint.

Note: If Vietnamese mint is not available, substitute with a mix of fresh coriander and mint.

Neapolitan chorizo puttanesca

hands-on time	20 mins
total time	40 mins
serves	3–4 as a main

(VE°)

Puttanesca uses simple ingredients that pack a serious flavour punch, playing off the combination of garlic, capers, chilli, and olives. I prefer mine Neapolitan-style, without the commonly used anchovies. Here I go for rigatoni or penne, but spaghetti would be equally good. This recipe will quickly find its place in your repertoire, as its taste:time ratio is hard to beat.

To make the sauce, heat the olive oil in a large, deep frying pan over medium heat. Add the onion and sauté for 5 minutes, until starting to soften. Add the garlic, chorizo, rosemary and mushrooms. Sauté for a further 3 minutes, until the onion is translucent and the garlic is golden brown. Add the chilli flakes, paprika, capers and olives and cook for a further 2 minutes, tossing together. Pour in the verjuice, bring to the boil and simmer for 2 minutes. Add the tomatoes and tomato paste, return to the boil, then reduce the heat to medium-low and simmer for 20–25 minutes, stirring once or twice, to allow the sauce to reduce and thicken nicely.

Meanwhile, for the pasta, bring a large saucepan of water with 1 tbsp salt to the boil over high heat. Add the pasta and cook for 8–10 minutes or as per packet instructions, until al dente. Drain, reserving 60ml of the pasta cooking water. Return the drained pasta to the saucepan.

To finish the sauce, stir in the parsley and pepper and simmer for a further minute. Stir the sauce through the cooked pasta and add the reserved pasta cooking water, tossing to coat. Adjust seasoning to taste with extra salt if desired.

Serve immediately, topped with extra chopped parsley and parmesan.

Vegan option: Use wedges of aubergine in place of chorizo, and leave out the grated parmesan or replace with a vegan alternative.

Ingredients

3 tbsp olive oil

1 red onion, finely chopped

4 cloves garlic, finely chopped

200g chorizo, cut in half lengthways and cut into 1cm slices

1 small sprig rosemary, leaves picked

150g white button mushrooms, sliced

1 tsp chilli flakes

1 tsp ground paprika

1 ½ tbsp capers

50g green pitted olives

125ml verjuice (or white wine)

400g can chopped tomatoes

4 tbsp tomato paste

1 tbsp sea salt

500g dried rigatoni or penne

1 small bunch (10g) flat-leaf parsley, leaves picked and finely chopped, plus extra to serve

½ tsp cracked black pepper

sea salt, extra, to taste

finely grated parmesan, to serve

Comfort

Slow & thoughtful mains

Food is a big part of birthdays in my whānau. For many, birthday food is all about puttin' on the ritz – and so it should be! I was fortunate that growing up, each birthday I was asked the question of what I wanted to have (within reason) for my birthday dinner. For me, there was only ever one answer to that question: 'PEA – PIE – PUD'. Pea-pie-pud is a kiwi classic, the combination of a meat pie (Jimmy's Pies from Roxburgh were the pie of choice), boiled peas and mashed potatoes. For 10-year-old me, it was the birthday dinner of my dreams. In fact, even as an adult, it's pretty hard to beat. That combination of creamy potatoes, sweet bursts of green, and rich flowing gravy was warming, savoury comfort food at its best.

Time and time again, we find ourselves drawn back to comfort food more than any other. Food that gets deep into your soul and fills you with a supreme pleasure. For many, this can be a shot of pure edible nostalgia, intoxicating in its cosy familiarity. For others it might be the qualities of the food itself, whether creamy or crunchy, meaty or moreish. Comfort also comes from the process behind the prize: the tactility of rubbing, rolling and crimping pastry for a Sunday family pie or the slow burn of roasted vegetables or meats, where only time can create the tender succulence I love.

Comfort can be as much about healing as it is about satisfaction. It doesn't take much to realise the restorative qualities of comfort foods, both in nutrition and gesture: a warm embrace from your grandmother's chicken soup; a spoonful of the neighbour's homemade apple crumble. Home-cooked expressions of care and compassion, comfort food that heals.

Within this chapter are recipes that explore what comfort food can and ought to be, each with their own unique twists. The Beetroot blush lasagne (page 137) may be vegetarian, but gives you all those warming layers of rich deliciousness that you want from its usually meat-based counterpart. Childhood memories of pepper steak pies, flaky pastry and food court curries with Dad manifest in the Black pepper & paneer pie with mango salsa (page 142). Then of course there are some foods that scream universal comfort, and it's hard to look past the Ultimate vegan burgers (page 164) or Fennel-pepper fried chicken with spicy mandarin sauce (page 167). Recipes that require a little extra love and attention but will hit that comfort spot where it counts.

This is food that awakens the soul. Food that raises the morale. Food that melts the heart.

hands-on time	40 mins
total time	2 hours
serves	8 as a main

Beetroot blush lasagne

Beetroot béchamel

1kg beetroot, peeled and chopped into 2cm chunks

3 tbsp olive oil

100g butter

100g plain flour

1 litre milk

¼ tsp ground nutmeg

¾ tsp sea salt

¾ tsp cracked black pepper

Filling

750g peeled pumpkin flesh (from ½ crown pumpkin), chopped into 2cm chunks

1 tsp ground cumin

2 tbsp finely chopped sage

5 tbsp olive oil

6 cloves garlic, finely chopped

200g spinach leaves, shredded

200g feta, crumbled

½ tsp cracked black pepper

Additional ingredients

375g fresh or instant dried lasagne sheets

2 large handfuls grated Tasty cheese

This is no ordinary vegetarian lasagne. Roasted beetroot is blitzed through béchamel and layered with pockets of pumpkin, spinach, sage and feta. It can be made in advance and heated as the occasion beckons.

Preheat the oven to 180°C fan-forced (or 200°C conventional). Line 2 large oven trays with baking paper.

First roast the beetroot and pumpkin. In a bowl, toss the beetroot with 3 tbsp olive oil and season generously with salt and pepper. Tip out onto one oven tray. In a clean bowl, toss the pumpkin with the ground cumin, 1 tbsp of the sage, 3 tbsp of the olive oil and season with salt and pepper. Tip onto the other tray. Roast the beetroot for about 50 minutes, until cooked through (a knife should easily pierce through the flesh). Roast the pumpkin for 30 minutes or until tender. Remove the roasted beetroot and pumpkin from the oven and reduce the oven temperature to 160°C fan-forced (or 180°C conventional).

For the beetroot béchamel, melt the butter in a large, deep saucepan over medium heat until starting to bubble and foam. Add the flour and whisk for a minute or two, until it forms a thick smooth paste. Remove from the heat and gradually pour in the milk, whisking constantly until the mixture is smooth. Return to medium heat and slowly bring to the boil. Cook for about 5 minutes, stirring regularly to prevent the sauce catching on the bottom of the pan, until nicely thickened. Remove from the heat and add the roasted beetroot, nutmeg, salt and pepper. Using a stick blender (or similar), blitz until completely smooth.

For the filling, heat the remaining 2 tbsp olive oil in a frying pan over medium heat. Add the garlic and sauté for 2 minutes, until starting to brown. Add the spinach and cook for a couple of minutes, until it is just starting to wilt. Transfer to a large bowl and toss together with the roast pumpkin, remaining sage, feta and pepper.

To construct the lasagne, lightly grease a deep ovenproof dish or baking tin (about 33cm x 23cm) with butter. Spread a very thin layer of beetroot béchamel over the base of the dish. Arrange a single layer of lasagne sheets over the béchamel, then spread with half the filling. Add another layer of lasagne sheets and spread with half the béchamel and a handful of grated Tasty cheese. Repeat so that you have 4 layers of lasagne sheets, with a top layer of béchamel sprinkled with Tasty cheese. Bake for 40–45 minutes, until golden brown and the lasagne sheets are cooked through. Remove from the oven and leave to cool for 5 minutes.

Serve warm, with your favourite side salad.

Legendary lamb shanks with mint gremolata & saffron mash

hands-on time	45 mins
total time	3 hours 20 mins
serves	4 as a main

GF

Not long after my partner and I started dating, I took him on a mystery evening out of the city, where I cooked these Moroccan-style lamb shanks with rose water, apricots and olives. I like to think it was this meal that won him over, and here we are still together.

Preheat the oven to 150°C fan-forced (or 170°C conventional).

For the lamb shanks, toast the seeds and peppercorns in a large frying pan over medium heat for 1–2 minutes, until fragrant and starting to colour and pop. Use a mortar and pestle to grind the toasted seeds to a reasonably fine powder. Add the ground spices and set aside.

Pat the lamb shanks dry with a paper towel and season with sea salt and pepper. Heat 2 tbsp of the oil in the frying pan over medium-high heat. Add the lamb shanks and cook for 5 minutes, turning so they brown on all sides. Transfer to a large casserole dish or Dutch oven with a lid.

Heat the remaining 2 tbsp oil in the pan and sauté the onion for 5 minutes, until starting to soften and become translucent. Add the garlic, lemon zest, lemon juice and spice mixture. Fry for a further minute to coat the onion. Pour in the verjuice, increase the heat to high and bring to the boil. Once starting to bubble, remove from the heat and add to the casserole dish with the lamb shanks. Add the stock, rose water, olives, dried apricots and sea salt. Stir to coat the meat. Cover and cook in the oven for 3 hours, turning the shanks and spooning the sauce over the meat every hour, until the meat is tender and almost falling off the bone.

To prepare the mint gremolata, place all the ingredients in a bowl and toss to combine. Refrigerate to allow the flavours to amalgamate.

For the saffron mash, place the potatoes in a large saucepan and cover with cold water. Add 1 tbsp salt and bring to the boil over high heat. Cook for about 20 minutes or until cooked through (a knife should go through each potato easily). Meanwhile, heat the milk in a small saucepan over medium heat until it just comes to a simmer. Stir in the saffron threads and garlic. Remove from the heat and set aside to infuse. Drain the potatoes and return to the pan. Place over medium heat for 30 seconds, stirring the potatoes to roughen the edges up a little. Remove from the heat and blitz with a stick blender or mash until fully smooth. Return the mash to low heat, and stir for

Lamb shanks

1 tsp fennel seeds

1 tsp black mustard seeds

1 tsp cumin seeds

½ tsp black peppercorns

1 tsp ground cinnamon

1 tsp ground cardamom

½ tsp ground turmeric

4 lamb shanks (about 450g each)

4 tbsp olive oil

1 brown onion, finely chopped

2 cloves garlic, finely chopped

finely grated zest and freshly squeezed juice of 1 lemon

250ml verjuice or white wine

375ml vegetable stock

2 tbsp rose water

12 pitted black olives

100g dried apricots, halved

1 tsp sea salt

Mint gremolata

4 tbsp finely chopped parsley leaves

2 tbsp finely chopped mint leaves

2 cloves garlic, finely grated

finely grated zest and freshly squeezed juice of 1 lemon

Saffron mash

1kg agria potatoes, peeled and cut into 3–4cm chunks

1 tbsp + ½ tsp sea salt

60ml milk

¼ tsp saffron threads

1 clove garlic, finely grated

100g chilled butter, cubed

½ tsp cracked black pepper

2 minutes to dry the mash out a little. Remove from the heat and add the butter, whipping quickly with a wooden spoon until the butter is melted into the mash. Add the infused milk (saffron strands and all) a little at a time, whipping after each addition until combined. Blitz or mash again to smooth out any remaining lumps then stir in the pepper and remaining ½ tsp salt, adjusting to taste.

To serve, spoon a bed of saffron mash onto each plate and place a lamb shank on top. Spoon over a generous amount of sauce and sprinkle with the mint gremolata.

Note: You could cook the lamb shanks in a slow cooker on LOW for 8–10 hours or HIGH for 6 hours, until tender and almost falling off the bone. Ensure you still brown the meat and prepare the sauce as above before placing in the slow cooker.

Stuffed aubergines with crimson sauce & green caper oil

hands-on time	50 mins
total time	1 hour 15 mins
serves	4–5 as a main

(GF)

This recipe uses an Ottolenghi-inspired technique. Aubergines are sliced into steaks, roasted, then rolled up to enclose a ricotta and spinach filling before being baked in a tomato-based sauce and doused in a zingy caper oil.

Preheat the oven to 200°C fan-forced (or 220°C conventional). Line 2 large oven trays with baking paper.

First roast the aubergines and capsicums. Brush each side of the aubergine slices with the olive oil. Arrange in a single layer on the oven trays and sprinkle with ½ tsp each of salt and pepper. Place the capsicum halves next to the aubergines, also in a single layer. Roast for 30 minutes, turning the vegetables over halfway through, until soft. Set aside to cool while you make the sauce. Reduce the oven temperature to 180°C fan-forced (or 200°C conventional).

For the crimson sauce, heat the olive oil in a large frying pan over medium heat. Add the onion and sauté for 5 minutes until starting to soften. Add the garlic, paprika, cinnamon and brown sugar. Cook for 2 minutes or until starting to caramelise. Add the red wine and simmer for 1 minute to deglaze the pan, then add the remaining ingredients (except the capsicums and parmesan) and 125ml water. Increase the heat to medium-high and bring to the boil. Reduce to medium-low and simmer for 15 minutes, stirring occasionally, until the sauce has reduced and thickened a little. Remove from the heat and transfer the sauce to a large bowl. Add the roasted capsicum halves and using a stick blender (or similar), blitz the sauce until relatively smooth. Transfer the sauce to a baking dish or cast iron pan about 25cm in diameter.

For the stuffed aubergines, place the spinach leaves in a bowl and cover with boiling water. Leave for 2 minutes then drain the water, rinse with cold water, drain again, then squeeze out any excess water from the leaves. Finely chop the blanched spinach and return to the bowl. Add the ricotta, parmesan, lemon zest, parsley and remaining salt and pepper and mix to combine. Dollop 1 tbsp of the ricotta mixture at one end of an aubergine slice and roll up the aubergine to enclose. Repeat with remaining aubergine and filling. Gently place seam side-down into the sauce, forming a single layer (the tops of the aubergines will be poking out). Sprinkle with the parmesan. Bake for 20–25 minutes, until the parmesan is golden and the sauce is bubbling. Remove from the oven and leave to rest for 5 minutes.

Stuffed aubergines

2 medium–large aubergines (about 700g total), cut lengthways into 1cm-thick slices

60ml olive oil

1 tsp sea salt

1 tsp cracked black pepper

100g baby spinach leaves

250g ricotta

2 tbsp grated parmesan

finely grated zest of ½ lemon

1 small handful flat-leaf parsley leaves, finely chopped

Crimson sauce

2 medium–large red capsicums, halved, cored and deseeded

2 tbsp olive oil

1 red onion, finely chopped

4 cloves garlic, finely chopped

1 ½ tsp ground paprika

½ tsp ground cinnamon

1 tsp soft brown sugar

60ml red wine

400g can chopped tomatoes

4 tbsp tomato paste

1 tbsp finely chopped oregano leaves

1 tbsp finely chopped basil leaves

1 tsp balsamic vinegar

1 tsp sea salt

½ tsp cracked black pepper

1 handful grated parmesan, to sprinkle

Green caper oil

1 tbsp capers

freshly squeezed juice of
½ lemon

60ml olive oil

1 tsp honey

¼ tsp sea salt

1 green chilli, finely chopped

1 large handful flat-leaf parsley
leaves, chopped

To make the green caper oil, place all the ingredients in a jar or bowl and blitz with a stick blender (or similar) until well-blended. Alternatively, finely chop the capers, chilli and parsley and mix with the remaining ingredients.

To serve, drizzle the stuffed aubergines generously with the green caper oil and serve warm with salad greens and fresh bread or pasta.

Black pepper & paneer pie with mango salsa

hands-on time	1 hour
total time	2 hours
serves	6–8 as a main

Pies and curries are my ultimate comfort foods, so it seemed only right to give you both. The earthy warmth in the filling comes from a hefty dose of black pepper. Depending on seasonal availability, you can substitute pumpkin with kūmara.

Preheat the oven to 180°C fan-forced (or 200°C conventional). Grease the base and sides of a 23cm round springform tin generously with butter.

For the filling, place a large, deep frying pan over medium heat. Once hot, add the peppercorns, cumin and coriander seeds and toast for a minute or two until fragrant. Use a mortar and pestle to grind to a fine powder. Heat the coconut oil in the frying pan over medium heat. Add the onion and sauté for 8 minutes, stirring occasionally, until softened. Add the pumpkin and cook for 5 minutes until the edges are starting to caramelise. Stir in the ginger, garlic, cardamom pods and cinnamon stick. Fry for a couple of minutes, then add the garam masala, amchur, turmeric, tomato paste and ground toasted spices, tossing through the vegetables for a minute. Add the coconut cream, peas and salt. Bring to a simmer and cook for about 10 minutes, stirring occasionally so the sauce doesn't stick to the bottom of the pan, until the pumpkin is just cooked through and the sauce has thickened. Stir through the paneer and coriander leaves, and simmer for a further 2 minutes. Season to taste and discard the cinnamon stick. Transfer to a large bowl to cool completely.

To assemble the pie, take the chilled rough puff pastry, cut off one-third and set aside (this will become the top). On a lightly floured surface, roll the larger portion of pastry to a large round big enough to cover the base and sides of the tin (about 35cm diameter). Carefully place the rolled pastry into the greased tin, pressing gently into the base and sides and trimming any excess pastry so it is level with the rim of the tin. Spoon the filling into the pastry. Roll out the reserved pastry to a round large enough to cover the filling. Carefully place the pastry on top of the filling and press into the top edge of the pastry sides, using your thumb or a fork to seal. Brush the top of the pastry evenly with the whisked egg and scatter with the poppy seeds. Place the tin on an oven tray and bake for about 40 minutes until the pastry is golden brown. Set aside for 10 minutes to cool slightly before removing from the tin.

1 quantity rough puff pastry, chilled (page 229)

1 egg, lightly whisked

1 tbsp poppy seeds

Black pepper & paneer filling

1 tbsp black peppercorns

1 tsp coriander seeds

1 tsp cumin seeds

2 tbsp coconut oil

2 brown onions, finely chopped

500g peeled pumpkin flesh, chopped into 2cm chunks

1 tbsp finely grated fresh ginger

4 cloves garlic, finely chopped

4 green cardamom pods

1 cinnamon stick

2 tsp garam masala

1 tsp amchur

1 tsp ground turmeric

2 tbsp tomato paste

400ml can coconut cream

200g frozen peas

1 ½ tsp sea salt

350g paneer, chopped into 2cm cubes

2 tbsp chopped coriander leaves

Mango salsa

2 tsp black mustard seeds

2 tsp poppy seeds

flesh of 1 large ripe mango, chopped into small cubes

1 small red capsicum, cored, deseeded and diced

½ red onion, finely chopped

½ red chilli, finely chopped

1 large handful coriander leaves, chopped

freshly squeezed juice of 1 lime

½ tsp sea salt

¼ tsp ground cardamom

Make the mango salsa as the pie bakes. In a small frying pan over medium heat, toast the black mustard and poppy seeds for a minute or so until starting to pop. Transfer to a bowl, add the remaining salsa ingredients and toss to combine. Set aside to allow the flavours to infuse.

Serve the pie warm, with a generous serving of mango salsa on the side.

Baked orzo with caramelised pears, lemon, basil & feta

hands-on time	45 mins
total time	1 hour
serves	4–5 as a main

While orzo (also known as risoni) is often made on the stovetop, I've opted to bake it for extra deliciousness. The combination of sweet pear with the salty feta and lemony pasta is everything.

Preheat the oven to 180°C fan-forced (or 200°C conventional).

For the baked orzo, cut the leek in half lengthways then cut into 1cm slices. Melt the butter over medium heat in a Dutch oven or flameproof casserole dish (about 25cm diameter). Add the leek, onion and salt and sauté for 15 minutes until softened and starting to caramelise. Stir in the garlic, grated pear, fennel seeds and orzo. Cook for 2 minutes. Pour in the white wine and let simmer for 1 minute, then add the stock and bring to the boil. Remove from the heat and stir in the mustard, basil, pepper, lemon zest and the juice of 1 lemon.

Cover with the lid and bake for 15 minutes. While the orzo is baking, place the broad beans in a heatproof bowl, cover with boiling water and leave for 3 minutes. Drain and rinse under cold water. Pop the broad beans out of their husks so you are left with the tender bright green beans.

Remove the orzo from the oven and add the broad beans, juice of the remaining lemon and the zucchini. Crumble in 100g of the feta and stir to combine. Season with extra salt to taste if needed, then return to the oven and bake for a further 10 minutes, until the orzo is cooked and vegetables have softened. Uncover and bake for a final 10 minutes, until the liquid has been absorbed and the edges are turning golden. Remove from the oven and leave to stand for 5 minutes.

Meanwhile, for the caramelised pears, melt the butter in a frying pan over medium heat. Add the sliced pear and cook for 5 minutes, until starting to soften. Add the sugar, cinnamon and salt, and cook for a couple more minutes until the pear slices are soft and caramelised.

To serve, spoon the caramelised pears and syrup evenly over the top of the baked orzo. Crumble over the remaining feta and finish with a little extra chopped fresh basil. Serve warm.

---

1 large leek, white and pale green part only

30g butter

1 red onion, thinly sliced

½ tsp sea salt

6 cloves garlic, finely chopped

1 pear, cored and coarsely grated

1 tsp fennel seeds

300g orzo

125ml white wine

625ml vegetable stock

1 tsp Dijon mustard

2 large handfuls basil leaves, finely shredded, plus extra to serve

1 tsp cracked black pepper

finely grated zest of 1 lemon

freshly squeezed juice of 2 lemons

200g fresh or frozen podded broad beans

1 zucchini, halved lengthways and thinly sliced

150g feta

Caramelised pears

50g butter

1 large pear (such as Beurre Bosc), halved, cored and thinly sliced

1 tbsp soft brown sugar

½ tsp ground cinnamon

¼ tsp sea salt

hands-on time	15 mins
total time	2 hours 30 mins
serves	4 as a main

(GF)

Slow-braised orange & coriander beef curry

1 tbsp coriander seeds

1 tbsp poppy seeds

2 tsp cumin seeds

2 tsp fennel seeds

2 tsp yellow mustard seeds

2 tbsp coconut or canola oil

2 brown onions, thinly sliced

5 cloves garlic, finely chopped

1 long red chilli, finely chopped

2 tsp ground turmeric

2 tsp garam masala

1 tsp ground ginger

800g chuck or blade steak, fat trimmed, cut into 2–3cm chunks

1 tsp sea salt

1 tsp cracked black pepper

finely grated zest of 2 oranges

400ml can coconut cream

400g can chopped tomatoes

2 tbsp tomato paste

freshly squeezed juice of 2 oranges (about 120ml)

To serve

coconut rice (page 215)

coriander leaves

unsweetened natural yoghurt, optional

Slowly cooking in the oven allows the beef to braise and tenderise while the flavours deepen. If the meat starts to stick to the casserole dish towards the end of cooking, stir through a splash of water to loosen the sauce a little. Serve with coconut rice (page 215).

Preheat the oven to 160°C fan-forced (or 180°C conventional).

To make the curry, heat a small frying pan over medium–high heat. Add the coriander, poppy, cumin, fennel and mustard seeds. Toast the seeds for a minute or two, until fragrant and starting to crackle. Use a mortar and pestle to grind the toasted seeds to a reasonably fine powder. Heat the oil in a 24cm Dutch oven or flameproof casserole dish over medium heat and add the onion. Sauté for 5 minutes, until starting to soften. Add the garlic and chilli and fry for a further minute. Stir in the ground seeds, turmeric, garam masala and ginger. Add the beef, salt and pepper and cook for 3–4 minutes, until lightly browned. Stir in the orange zest and cook for a further 30 seconds.

Remove from the heat and add the remaining ingredients, reserving half the orange juice. Stir through to coat the meat. Cover and bake for 2–2 ½ hours, stirring halfway through, until the meat is tender and sauce has thickened.

To serve, stir through the reserved orange juice and adjust seasoning to taste. Serve with coconut rice, coriander leaves and a dollop of yoghurt, if desired.

Butternut & aubergine snake with basil & pistachio pesto

hands-on time	45 mins
total time	1 hour 45 mins
serves	4–6 as a main

(VE) S A

Before it is rolled, the snake will be very long (more than a metre), so make sure you have plenty of bench space cleared before assembly, and perhaps a second pair of hands to help with the rolling.

Preheat the oven to 180°C fan-forced (or 200°C conventional). Line 2 oven trays with baking paper.

First roast the vegetables for the filling. Toss the pumpkin, aubergine, sumac, sage, salt, pepper, maple syrup and 4 tbsp of the olive oil together in a large bowl to coat the vegetables evenly. Transfer to one oven tray, spreading out in a single layer. Roast for 25–30 minutes, until golden brown and cooked through (a knife should easily pierce the vegetables).

Meanwhile, for the basil & pistachio pesto, place the pistachios onto the second tray and roast for 8 minutes until deeply fragrant and starting to brown. Cool slightly, then set aside 1 tbsp for decorating. Place the remaining roasted pistachios in a food processor with the basil, garlic, lemon zest and juice, capers, pepper and salt. Pulse to form a chunky paste. Gradually drizzle in the olive oil, pulsing a few times, until combined. Add extra lemon juice or salt to taste. Set aside 2 tbsp of the pesto for serving.

To finish the filling, heat the remaining 2 tbsp olive oil in a large frying pan over medium heat. Add the onion and sauté for 15 minutes, stirring occasionally, until softened and starting to caramelise. Add the garlic

500g peeled butternut pumpkin flesh, cut into 1cm chunks

1 aubergine (about 300g), cut into 1cm chunks

1 tbsp ground sumac

1 tbsp finely chopped sage leaves

1 tsp sea salt

½ tsp cracked black pepper

2 tbsp maple syrup

6 tbsp olive oil, plus extra for assembly

3 brown onions, thinly sliced

4 cloves garlic, finely chopped

100g baby spinach leaves

2 tbsp finely chopped flat-leaf parsley leaves

9 large sheets vegan filo pastry (about 40cm x 30cm)

Basil & pistachio pesto

115g pistachio kernels

80g (2 packed cups) basil leaves

4 cloves garlic, finely chopped

finely grated zest and freshly squeezed juice of 1 lemon

1 tbsp capers

½ tsp cracked black pepper

½ tsp sea salt

125ml olive oil, plus extra to serve

and spinach leaves and cook for two minutes, stirring through the onion until the spinach is wilted. Transfer to a large bowl. Add the roasted vegetables to the onion and spinach. Add the chopped parsley and toss to evenly combine. Set aside to cool. Reduce the oven to 160°C fan-forced (or 180°C conventional). Line a large oven tray with clean baking paper.

To assemble the snake, take three sheets of filo pastry and place on a wide clean work surface with the long sides facing towards you. Brush the sheets with olive oil then overlap each sheet by 5cm, to form one long continuous rectangle. Place three more sheets of filo on top, again brushing and overlapping. Repeat once more with the remaining three sheets of pastry to form a long 3-layer rectangle, with the long side facing towards you. Brush the pastry lightly with a little extra oil to finish. Dollop spoonfuls of basil & pistachio pesto along the long side of the pastry closest to you. Using the back of the spoon, spread the pesto into an even layer, 10cm wide, along the entire edge. Spoon the vegetable filling on top of the pesto, placing evenly along the entire length. Carefully but confidently, taking the long edge facing towards you, roll the pastry up and away from you to enclose the filling. You will need to start at one end and move back and forth along the length of the pastry, gradually rolling it up as you go (if you have a second person to help you, this makes things a lot easier). With the seam side down, slowly curl the snake into a loose spiral – it is okay if the pastry cracks a little in some places. Carefully transfer the spiralled snake to the oven tray and brush the top evenly with olive oil. Bake for 50–60 minutes, until the pastry is crisp and golden. Set aside to cool for 5 minutes.

To serve, mix a little extra olive oil into the reserved pesto so it is a drizzling consistency. Roughly chop the reserved roasted pistachios. Brush the top of the filo snake with any oil that has leaked out during baking, and carefully transfer the snake to a serving platter. Drizzle with the pesto and sprinkle with the chopped pistachios. Serve warm.

Beetroot & jackfruit chilli with sour yoghurt

hands-on time	20 mins
total time	1 hour 40 mins
serves	4–6 as a main

(VE) (GF) S S A W

Jackfruit is a popular substitute for pulled pork, due to its hearty, fibrous texture and ability to absorb flavours. This chilli is full of vegetable goodness, warming spices and earthy richness. The sour yoghurt is my spin on the classic pairing of sour cream – it's a plant-based substitute that I find still brings that creamy acidity.

Preheat the oven to 160°C fan-forced (or 180°C conventional).

First make the sour yoghurt. Place all ingredients in a bowl and whisk together until smooth and combined. Cover and refrigerate until ready to serve.

To prepare the chilli, heat the oil in a large Dutch oven or flameproof casserole dish over medium heat. Add the onion, capsicum, carrot and 1 tsp salt. Sauté for 10 minutes, or until the onion and capsicum are nicely softened. Stir in the mushroom, beetroot and garlic and cook for 3 minutes. Add the ground spices and cook for a further minute, tossing through the vegetables. Add the remaining ingredients (including 1 tsp salt) and 250ml water, stirring to combine evenly. Bring to the boil. Cover and bake for 1 hour 20 minutes, until nicely thickened and the jackfruit is tender and falling apart. Transfer the jackfruit pieces to a chopping board and use two forks to shred. Return the shredded jackfruit to the chilli and stir through.

To serve, stir the lime juice through the chilli and adjust seasoning to taste. Spoon the warm chilli into deep bowls and top with a generous dollop of the sour yoghurt, pickled chillies and extra fresh coriander. Serve alone, or with rice or tortillas on the side.

Sour yoghurt

140g unsweetened natural Greek-style coconut yoghurt

1 tbsp apple cider vinegar

1 tbsp lemon juice

½ tsp Dijon mustard

½ tsp sea salt

Chilli

2 tbsp canola oil

2 red onions, thinly sliced

2 red or yellow capsicums, cored, deseeded and diced

1 carrot, peeled and finely chopped

2 tsp sea salt

150g mushrooms, finely chopped

1 beetroot (about 300g), peeled and coarsely grated

6 cloves garlic, finely chopped

2 tsp ground cumin

2 tsp ground paprika

1 tsp ground coriander

1 tsp ground cinnamon

1 tsp ground cayenne pepper

2 tsp dried oregano

1 tbsp cocoa powder

565g can young green jackfruit, rinsed and drained

400g can kidney beans, rinsed and drained

2 x 400g cans chopped tomatoes

3 tbsp tomato paste

2 tbsp chopped coriander leaves

1 tbsp gluten-free soy sauce
1 tbsp soft brown sugar
To serve
freshly squeezed juice of 1 lime
pickled chillies (page 218)
fresh coriander leaves
tortillas or rice, if desired

Larb-stuffed kūmara with crispy shallots & sticky rice

hands-on time	55 mins
total time	1 hour 15 mins
serves	4 as a main

(VE°) (GF)

Larb is traditionally made with ground meat, but this version uses tofu, and stuffing the larb into roasted whole kūmara makes it a filling main.

Preheat the oven to 200°C fan-forced (or 220°C conventional). Line a large oven tray with baking paper.

To start the sticky rice, place 250g of the glutinous rice in a bowl, cover with cold water and set aside to soak for 30 minutes.

Next, roast the kūmara. Place the whole kūmara on the oven tray and prick each one a few times with a fork. Roast for 55–60 minutes or until a knife goes easily through the flesh. Carefully cut the roasted kūmara down the centre lengthways, two-thirds of the way through so the bases remain intact. Leave to cool for 10 minutes.

Meanwhile, to cook the sticky rice, drain the rice and transfer to a medium saucepan. Add three kaffir lime leaves and 375ml cold water. Cover the saucepan with a lid, place over high heat and bring to the boil. As soon as the rice is bubbling vigorously, reduce the heat to low and leave to simmer for 12 minutes. Do NOT remove the lid during the cooking process. Remove from the heat and leave the rice to stand, with the lid still on, for 10 minutes.

For the crispy shallots, heat the canola oil in a small–medium frying pan over medium heat. Add the shallot and cook for 12–15 minutes, using a spatula to separate the rings as they cook and tossing occasionally, until a deep golden brown. Transfer to a paper towel-lined plate, spreading them out to drain and crisp as they cool.

For the tofu larb, toast the remaining rice in a frying pan over medium-high heat, stirring occasionally, until evenly golden. Use a mortar and pestle to grind the rice to a slightly coarse powder. Heat the coconut oil in the frying pan over medium heat. Finely slice the remaining two kaffir lime leaves and add to the pan with the shallot, lemongrass, ginger, garlic, chilli, lime zest and orange zest and fry for a minute. Crumble the tofu into the pan, add the salt and cook for 10 minutes, stirring regularly, until the tofu is lightly browned. In a bowl, whisk together the fish sauce, soy sauce, lime juice, orange juice and brown sugar. Add 4 tbsp of the dressing to the pan and cook for a couple of minutes to coat the tofu and absorb all of the liquid. Remove from the heat and transfer to a large bowl. Add the remaining dressing, spring onion, chopped herbs and ground rice. Stir through to combine. Taste and add more lime juice, sea salt or chilli as desired.

300g glutinous rice

4 orange kūmara (about 300g each)

5 kaffir lime leaves

2 tbsp coconut oil

2 shallots, finely chopped

1 stalk lemongrass, tough outer layers removed, end trimmed, very thinly sliced

1 tbsp finely grated fresh ginger

4 cloves garlic, finely grated

1 red chilli, finely chopped

finely grated zest of 1 lime

finely grated zest of ½ orange

300g firm tofu, drained

1 tsp sea salt

3 tbsp fish sauce

2 tbsp gluten-free light soy sauce

freshly squeezed juice of 2 limes

freshly squeezed juice of ½ orange

2 tbsp soft brown sugar

2 spring onions, ends trimmed, thinly sliced

1 large handful coriander leaves, roughly chopped, plus extra to serve

1 large handful mint leaves, roughly chopped, plus extra to serve

1 large handful Thai basil leaves, roughly chopped, plus extra to serve

Crispy shallots

60ml canola oil

4 small shallots, sliced as thinly as possible (on a mandoline)

To serve, place the warm kūmara on plates and spoon a generous amount of the tofu larb down the centre of each. Sprinkle with the crispy shallots and extra chopped herbs, and serve with sticky rice.

Vegan option: Use vegan fish sauce or more light soy sauce in place of regular fish sauce.

Herb, onion & hazelnut cheesecake with blistered tomatoes

hands-on time	1 hour
total time	3 hours
serves	6–8 as a main

Here, big herb and caramelised onion flavours hit through the light texture of the ricotta. This savoury cheesecake is best eaten at room temperature or even slightly warm, perfect for a long lunch with friends.

Preheat the oven to 160°C fan-forced (or 180°C conventional). Grease and line the base and sides of a 23cm round springform tin with baking paper. Line a rimmed oven tray with baking paper.

For the hazelnut base, place the hazelnuts onto the oven tray and roast for 12 minutes, until golden brown. Leave to cool for 5 minutes, then rub the hazelnuts with a tea towel to remove the skins. Transfer the roasted hazelnuts to a food processor, add the rolled oats and blitz to fine crumbs. Place into a large bowl. In a saucepan over medium-low heat, melt together the butter and honey. Pour onto the hazelnut mixture and stir to combine. Spread over the base of the prepared tin and use a flat bottomed glass to press firmly into an even layer. Bake for 10 minutes, until light golden brown. Set aside to cool while you make the filling.

Reduce the oven temperature to 150°C fan-forced (or 170°C conventional).

To make the filling, heat the olive oil in a large frying pan over medium heat. Add the onions and sauté for 20 minutes, stirring occasionally, until softened and starting to caramelise. Add the garlic, balsamic and sugar and cook for a further 5 minutes, until the onions are sticky. Transfer to a bowl and set aside to cool. In a food processor, blitz together the ricotta, parmesan, basil and parsley until relatively smooth and the herbs are finely chopped. Using an electric hand or stand mixer, beat the cream cheese in a large bowl until smooth. Add the ricotta mixture and beat until combined, scraping down the sides of the bowl to incorporate evenly. Add the eggs one at a time, beating after each addition, until combined and smooth. Stir through the lime zest, juice, salt and pepper.

To assemble the cheesecake, stand the springform tin on an oven tray (to catch any oils that may leak as it cooks). Spoon the cooled caramelised onions onto the hazelnut base, spreading out with the back of a spoon into an even layer. Pour the cheesecake filling over the onions, shaking the tin gently to level. Bake for 1 hour, until the sides of the cheesecake are set but the centre has a very slight wobble when shaken gently. Turn off the oven, open the door slightly, and leave the cheesecake to cool for 30 minutes in the turned off oven. Remove from the oven, release the sides of the springform tin and remove the baking paper. Leave for at least 30 minutes, to cool completely to room temperature.

Hazelnut base

225g hazelnuts

55g traditional wholegrain rolled oats

100g butter

1 tbsp honey

Filling

2 tbsp olive oil

3 red onions, thinly sliced

4 cloves garlic, finely chopped

2 tbsp balsamic vinegar

1 tbsp soft brown sugar

500g ricotta

100g parmesan, finely grated

40g basil leaves

20g flat-leaf parsley leaves

250g cream cheese, at room temperature, chopped

4 eggs

finely grated zest and freshly squeezed juice of 2 limes

¾ tsp sea salt

¾ tsp cracked black pepper

Blistered tomatoes

2 tbsp olive oil

200g cherry tomatoes

2 cloves garlic, finely grated

1 tbsp red wine vinegar

½ tsp sea salt

½ tsp cracked black pepper

1 tbsp finely chopped basil leaves

freshly squeezed juice of ½ lime

When the cheesecake is almost cool, prepare the blistered tomatoes.
Heat the olive oil in a large frying pan over medium–high heat. Add the cherry tomatoes in a single layer and cook, undisturbed, for 2 minutes. Add the garlic, red wine vinegar, salt and pepper and cook for a further 2 minutes, tossing through the tomatoes. Remove from the heat, transfer to a bowl and add the chopped basil and lime juice, stirring gently to combine.

To serve, carefully run a large palette knife between the base of the cheesecake and the tin, to loosen. Slide the cheesecake onto a serving platter and spoon over the warm blistered tomatoes and juices. Top with a few extra basil leaves and serve in generous slices.

Butternut gnocchi with roasted capsicum sauce & chilli-garlic walnuts

hands-on time	45 mins
total time	1 hour 45 mins
serves	3–4 as a main

(VE)   (S) (A) (W)

Homemade gnocchi is a lot easier to make than you might think. 'oo' flour is more finely ground than plain flour and makes for a lighter and softer gnocchi; it is found at most specialty or wholefoods stores.

Preheat the oven to 180°C fan-forced (or 200°C conventional). Line 2 large oven trays with baking paper.

First roast the vegetables for the gnocchi and sauce. Place the whole potatoes on one of the oven trays and prick each one a few times with a fork. Bake for 30 minutes. Meanwhile, toss the chopped pumpkin in a bowl with the olive oil. Once the potatoes have been baking for 30 minutes, add the pumpkin to the oven tray with the potatoes and place the capsicums and garlic cloves for the sauce onto the other oven tray. Roast for 40 minutes, until the pumpkin and potatoes are both cooked through (a knife should go through easily) and the capsicums are soft. Remove from the oven and leave to cool until you can handle the potatoes.

Next make the roasted capsicum sauce to allow the flavours to infuse. Squeeze the roasted garlic from the skins into a food processor, and add the roasted capsicums and remaining sauce ingredients. Blitz until smooth, then set aside.

For the butternut gnocchi, place the roasted pumpkin in a large bowl and mash with a fork until relatively smooth. Using your hands, remove the skins from the potatoes. Press the flesh through a potato ricer or sieve into the bowl with the pumpkin. Mix gently to combine (the total weight should be about 450g). In a separate bowl, sift together the flour, 1 tsp salt, pepper, nutmeg and cinnamon. Add the dry ingredients to the pumpkin and potato mixture and gently mix with a wooden spoon until it just comes together to form a soft dough. Be careful not to overmix, or the gnocchi could end up being tough.

Bring a large saucepan of water with the remaining 1 tbsp sea salt to the boil over high heat while you roll out the gnocchi. Tip the dough out onto a floured surface and divide into three equal pieces. Using lightly floured hands, form each piece of dough into a log about 2cm thick and 40cm long. Cut each log into 2cm-wide pieces, dusting with a little extra flour as you go to prevent the gnocchi from sticking to the work surface. If you like, use the back of a fork to make some gentle indentations on one side of each gnocchi. This will increase the surface area exposed to the sauce, but isn't totally necessary. Add one-third of the gnocchi to the salted boiling water and cook for 2–3 minutes, until they float to the surface. Use a slotted spoon to lift out the gnocchi and transfer to a large tray or platter. Repeat with the remaining gnocchi in two more batches.

Butternut gnocchi

500g agria potatoes (about 2), washed

450g peeled butternut pumpkin flesh, chopped into 3cm chunks

1 tbsp olive oil

200g '00' flour

1 tsp + 1 tbsp sea salt

½ tsp cracked black pepper

¼ tsp ground nutmeg

¼ tsp ground cinnamon

Roasted capsicum sauce

4 red capsicums, cored, deseeded and quartered

4 cloves garlic, unpeeled

1 small bunch (10g) flat-leaf parsley, leaves picked and finely chopped

3 tbsp olive oil

1 tbsp pomegranate molasses

1 tbsp red wine vinegar

1 tsp cracked black pepper

½ tsp sea salt

¼ tsp ground cinnamon

To serve

2 tbsp olive oil

65g walnuts, roughly chopped

2 cloves garlic, finely chopped

1 tsp chilli flakes

rocket leaves

To serve, heat the 2 tbsp olive oil in a frying pan over medium heat. Add the walnuts, garlic and chilli flakes, and cook for a few minutes until the nuts and garlic are turning golden brown. Remove from the heat. Place the roasted capsicum sauce in a large saucepan over medium heat and stir occasionally until warm and just bubbling. Remove from the heat, add the cooked gnocchi to the sauce and stir through to coat. Spoon gnocchi and sauce onto serving plates and serve topped with the walnuts and fresh rocket.

hands-on time	15 mins
total time	5 hours
serves	6–8

(GF)   (S) (A) (W)

Lazy-day pulled pork with apple & beetroot slaw

Pulled pork

1.5kg pork shoulder or leg, bone-in

2 tsp ground sumac

1 tsp ground chipotle chilli (or other chilli powder)

1 tsp ground ginger

1 tsp ground cumin

¼ tsp ground cloves

2 tbsp soft brown sugar

1 tbsp finely grated fresh ginger

4 cloves garlic, finely chopped

1 large green apple, grated

60ml apple cider vinegar

60ml golden rum

2 tbsp tomato paste

½ tsp sea salt

½ tsp cracked black pepper

2 red onions, thinly sliced

400ml can coconut cream

Apple & beetroot slaw

¼ red cabbage, shredded

1 large green apple, halved, cored, cut into matchsticks

1 small beetroot (about 125g), finely grated

70g unsweetened natural yoghurt

3 tbsp apple cider vinegar

freshly squeezed juice of 1 lemon

2 tbsp pomegranate molasses

2 tbsp chopped mint leaves

1 handful coriander leaves

This combination of pork and slaw can be stuffed into bao, tacos and flatbreads, or served with your favourite sides. A healthy swig of rum and grated green apple give the meat incredible flavour. Allowing the slaw to marinate 30 minutes in the fridge lets the cabbage soften just a little.

For the pulled pork, trim any excess fat or skin from the pork. Pat the meat dry with paper towel. Using a sharp knife, score the meat diagonally a few times, making cuts just 1cm deep. This lets the marinade penetrate the flesh. Place into a medium–large (about 25cm diameter) Dutch oven or casserole dish with a lid. In a bowl, whisk together the spices, sugar, ginger, garlic, apple, vinegar, rum, tomato paste, salt and pepper until well combined. Pour over the pork and massage into both sides of the meat. Cover with the lid and leave at room temperature for 1 hour to marinate.

Preheat the oven to 140°C fan-forced (or 160°C conventional). Add the onion and coconut cream to the meat and stir through to coat. Cover and cook for about 4 hours, until the meat is very tender and falling apart.

For the apple & beetroot slaw, combine all ingredients in a bowl and toss together. Refrigerate for 30 minutes.

To serve, transfer the pork to a chopping board. Using two forks, pull the meat into shreds. Return the pork to the casserole dish and mix through the sauce to absorb all the moisture and flavour. Serve warm with the apple & beetroot slaw, either on their own or stuffed into tacos, buns or flatbreads.

Note: Alternatively, cook the pork in a slow cooker on LOW for 8–10 hours or HIGH for 6 hours, until tender and falling apart. Ensure you still marinate the pork first for maximum flavour.

Herby ricotta balls with creamy spinach, walnut & lemon sauce

hands-on time	45 mins
total time	1 hour
serves	3-4 as a main

 S S A W

This is rich, simple and satisfying. I like to use verjuice (the non-alcoholic juice of unripe grapes) in the sauce for its sourness and acidity, but white wine will do fine.

Preheat the oven to 180°C fan-forced (or 200°C conventional).

First make the herby ricotta balls. Use your hands to mix the ingredients together in a bowl until well combined. Shape the mixture into 10 golf ball-sized balls (about 45g each). Place onto a plate and refrigerate until needed.

For the creamy spinach, walnut & lemon sauce, heat the oil in a large frying pan over medium heat. Add the onion and sauté for 5 minutes, until starting to soften. Add the spring onion, garlic, fennel seeds and butter. Cook for 3 minutes, then add the walnuts and sugar and cook for a further 3 minutes until the nuts are starting to caramelise. Remove from the heat and transfer to a large bowl.

Place the spinach leaves in a large heatproof bowl and cover with boiling water. Leave for 3 minutes then drain. Rinse with cold water, drain again, then squeeze out any excess water. Add the leaves to the walnut mixture. Pour in the cream, and using a stick blender (or similar), blitz until relatively smooth.

Return the creamy spinach mixture to the frying pan and place over medium-high heat. Add the stock and verjuice and bring to the boil. Reduce the heat to medium-low and simmer for 5 minutes. Stir in the lemon juice, salt, pepper and cannellini beans, and adjust seasoning to taste. Transfer the sauce to a baking dish about 25cm in diameter (or if using an ovenproof frying pan, leave the sauce in the pan). Place the ricotta balls into the spinach sauce, so that the tops of the balls are poking out the top. Sprinkle the parmesan over. Bake for 20–25 minutes, until the parmesan is golden brown and the sauce is bubbling. Remove from the oven and stand for 5 minutes.

To serve, melt the extra butter in a small frying pan over medium heat. Add the extra walnuts and cook for 2–3 minutes, until the butter is a deep golden brown. Be careful not to burn the butter or walnuts. Drizzle the melted butter and walnuts over the ricotta balls and top with the extra herbs. Serve warm.

Herby ricotta balls

250g ricotta

40g parmesan, finely grated

30g basil leaves, finely chopped

20g flat-leaf parsley leaves, finely chopped

finely grated zest of 1 lemon

1 egg

100g fine breadcrumbs

¼ tsp sea salt

½ tsp cracked black pepper

Creamy spinach, walnut & lemon sauce

2 tbsp olive oil

1 brown onion, finely chopped

1 spring onion, finely chopped

5 cloves garlic, finely chopped

½ tsp fennel seeds

50g butter

40g walnuts, roughly chopped

1 tsp soft brown sugar

200g baby spinach leaves

125ml cream

125ml vegetable stock

60ml verjuice or white wine

freshly squeezed juice of 1 lemon

¾ tsp sea salt

½ tsp cracked black pepper

400g can cannellini beans, rinsed and drained

Additional ingredients

1 handful finely grated parmesan

30g butter, extra

40g walnuts, roughly chopped, extra

finely chopped flat-leaf parsley leaves, extra, to serve

fresh basil leaves, extra, to serve

hands-on time	20 mins
total time	4 hours 20 mins
serves	4 as a main

Coffee & cardamom braised beef cheeks

1kg beef cheeks

2 tbsp olive oil

1 red onion, thinly sliced

1 carrot, peeled and finely diced

8 cloves garlic, finely chopped

2 tsp ground cardamom

1 tsp ground cinnamon

2 star anise

250ml beef or vegetable stock

250ml strong black coffee

125ml red wine

65g dried pitted dates, roughly chopped

4 tbsp tomato paste

3 tbsp balsamic vinegar

1 tbsp chopped rosemary leaves

1 tbsp muscovado sugar

1 tsp sea salt

1 tsp cracked black pepper

fresh cooked pasta (pappardelle or tagliatelle), to serve (page 214)

finely chopped flat-leaf parsley, to serve

Coffee is an excellent tenderiser of meat, and its acidity amplifies the flavour of the beef. I like to cook them in the oven for better caramelisation, but I've included slow cooker directions for convenience.

Preheat the oven to 140°C fan-forced (or 160°C conventional).

Prepare the beef cheeks. Cut off any fatty membrane from the meat. Pat dry with paper towel and season each side with salt and pepper. Heat 1 tbsp olive oil in a large frying pan over medium-high heat. Add the beef cheeks and sear for 1–2 minutes on each side until browned, then transfer to a medium–large (about 25cm diameter) Dutch oven or casserole dish with a lid. Return the frying pan to the stovetop, reduce the heat to medium, and heat the remaining 1 tbsp oil. Add the onion and sauté for 5 minutes, until starting to soften. Add the carrot and garlic and sauté for another 2 minutes, until the garlic is golden. Stir in the cardamom, cinnamon and star anise, and heat for 30 seconds. Transfer to the Dutch oven with the meat. Add the remaining ingredients (except the pasta and parsley) and stir to coat the meat in the liquid. Cover and cook for about 4 hours, stirring halfway through to loosen the edges of the sauce, until the meat is tender and falls apart easily when touched.

To serve, either serve the beef cheeks whole, or using two forks, pull the meat into large chunks. Serve the meat with the sauce over pasta and sprinkle with chopped parsley to finish.

Note: Alternatively, cook the beef cheeks in a slow cooker on LOW for 8–10 hours or HIGH for 6 hours until tender and falling apart. Ensure you still brown the meat and prepare the sauce as above before placing in the slow cooker.

Ultimate vegan burgers

hands-on time	1 hour
total time	1 hour
makes	6 large burgers

(VE)   S S A W

Both vegans and meat lovers can rejoice – here is the answer to our burger prayers! Gently press the tofu for the full 20 minutes, lest too much liquid get into the patty mixture. Serve with vegan burger buns (page 227) and coriander onions (page 219).

Preheat the oven to 160°C fan-forced (or 180°C conventional). Line an oven tray with baking paper.

For the ultimate patties, pat the tofu dry with paper towel, then wrap in a tea towel and place on a plate. Place a weight (such as a cast iron frying pan, or couple of cans on top of another plate) on top of the wrapped tofu and set aside for 20 minutes for the excess moisture to be gently pressed out.

In a large frying pan over medium heat, toast the fennel, coriander and cumin seeds for a minute or two, until fragrant. Use a mortar and pestle to grind to a relatively fine powder; set aside. Heat 1 tbsp olive oil in the frying pan over medium heat and add the onion. Sauté for 5 minutes, until starting to soften. Add the remaining oil, mushroom, beetroot, walnuts and garlic and cook for 5 minutes, until the mushroom is soft and the garlic and walnuts are golden. Remove from the heat and transfer to a fine mesh sieve set over a bowl. Set aside for 5 minutes to allow some of the excess liquid to drain away (don't press the mixture). In a separate large bowl, mash the drained chickpeas with a fork to a slightly chunky paste. Add the ground spices, ground chilli, soy sauce, lemon zest, parsley, mint and the mushroom mixture, tossing to combine. Finely crumble the tofu and add to the bowl along with the breadcrumbs, salt and pepper. Use your hands to mix until it all comes together (you may need an extra 1–2 tbsp of breadcrumbs, depending on how moist the mixture is) and adjust seasoning to taste. Form the mixture into 6 large patties (about 130g each, 2cm thick). Place the patties on the tray and refrigerate for 10 minutes.

For the burger sauce, place the aquafaba, mustard, lemon juice and garlic in a tall, narrow container. Using a stick blender, blitz for 20 seconds until the mixture is white and starting to become fluffy. While continuing to blend, gradually pour in the oil, little by little, moving the stick blender up and down to emulsify. Gradually it will form a thick mayonnaise-like consistency. Add the paprika, chilli, salt and pepper. Blitz until smooth and adjust seasoning to taste.

Ultimate patties

200g extra firm tofu, drained

2 tsp fennel seeds

2 tsp coriander seeds

2 tsp cumin seeds

2 tbsp olive oil

1 small red onion, finely chopped

4 portobello mushrooms (about 125g total), stalks removed, roughly chopped into 5mm pieces

1 beetroot (about 200g), peeled and finely grated

35g walnuts, roughly chopped

4 cloves garlic, finely chopped

400g can chickpeas, drained, aquafaba (liquid) reserved

½ tsp ground chilli

2 tbsp light soy sauce

finely grated zest of 1 lemon

2 tbsp finely chopped flat-leaf parsley leaves

1 tbsp finely chopped mint leaves

50g fine breadcrumbs

1 ½ tsp sea salt

½ tsp cracked black pepper

2 tbsp canola oil, for frying

Burger sauce

60ml reserved aquafaba

1 tsp Dijon mustard

2 tbsp lemon juice

4 cloves garlic, finely grated

185ml canola oil

1 tsp ground paprika

½ tsp ground chilli, optional

½ tsp sea salt

½ tsp cracked black pepper

To serve

6 burger buns (page 227)

coriander onions (page 219)

sliced dill pickles or gherkins

rocket leaves

To cook the patties, heat the canola oil in a large frying pan over medium heat. Cook the patties for 4–5 minutes on each side, being careful as you flip them, until golden and crispy (you may need to cook them in two batches). Return to the oven tray and bake for 10 minutes. Remove from the oven and change the oven function to grill. Split open the burger buns with a bread knife and lightly toast the cut side of each bun half under the grill until golden.

To assemble the burgers, place a large spoonful of coriander onions onto the bottom half of each bun. Place the patties on top of the onions, followed by the rocket leaves. Spread some of the burger sauce onto each of the bun tops, add a few sliced gherkins, and carefully place on top of each burger. Devour.

hands-on time	1 hour
total time	1 hour
	(+ overnight brining)
serves	4–5

Fennel-pepper fried chicken with spicy mandarin sauce

Fried chicken

1 tbsp black peppercorns

2 tsp fennel seeds

2 tsp coriander seeds

1.2kg chicken breast fillets, cut into pieces the size of a small fist

1 handful coriander leaves, plus extra to serve

1 tbsp chopped thyme

3 tbsp + 1 tsp sea salt

1 lemon, halved

400ml can coconut cream

450g plain flour

1 tsp ground chilli

canola oil, for deep-frying

Spicy mandarin sauce

1 tbsp canola oil

10 black peppercorns

3 cloves garlic, finely chopped

1 red chilli, finely chopped

1 tbsp finely grated fresh ginger

60ml maple syrup

3 tbsp malt vinegar

finely grated zest of 2 mandarins

60ml freshly squeezed mandarin juice

½ tsp sea salt

There's something therapeutic about making fried chicken and it's always worth the effort. The key to fried chicken is in the brine, as it keeps the chicken incredibly moist and optimises the flavour.

Brine the chicken in advance. Toast the peppercorns, fennel and coriander seeds in a small frying pan over medium-high heat for a minute, until fragrant. Use a mortar and pestle to grind half the toasted spices to a fine powder. Place into an airtight container and set aside for the coating. Place the remaining toasted spices in a large bowl and add the chicken, coriander, thyme, 3 tbsp salt and 500ml cold water. Squeeze some of the juice from the lemon halves into the water, add the lemon and stir the brine to coat the chicken. Cover and refrigerate for a minimum of 4 hours, but preferably overnight.

To make the spicy mandarin sauce, heat the oil in a small saucepan over medium heat. Add the peppercorns, garlic, chilli and ginger and fry for 2 minutes. Add the remaining ingredients, increase the heat to high and bring to the boil. Reduce the heat to medium and simmer for 5 minutes, so the sauce reduces and thickens slightly. Transfer to a bowl, leave to cool to room temperature then refrigerate for a minimum of 1 hour (or overnight). Strain before serving.

To cook the chicken, remove the chicken from the brine and pat dry with paper towel. Add 5cm oil (enough to just cover the chicken) to a medium–large saucepan or Dutch oven. Heat the oil over medium-high heat to reach 170–180°C. You can measure this with a thermometer or by dropping a piece of bread into the oil; if it sizzles, floats and quickly browns, the oil is ready.

Place three bowls beside the stove. Pour the coconut cream into one bowl. Separate the flour into the remaining two bowls, with 150g in one bowl and 300g in the other. Add the ground toasted spices to the 300g flour, along with the ground chilli and remaining 1 tsp salt. Line a large plate with paper towel and place beside the stove. Once the oil is at temperature, take a piece of chicken and coat with the plain flour, shaking off any excess. Dip the chicken into the coconut cream then into the spiced flour, again shaking off any excess. Gently place the coated chicken into the hot oil. Repeat with more chicken to fry in batches of 4 or 5 pieces, ensuring they form a single layer in the oil. Cook for 10 minutes, turning once or twice, until golden brown and cooked through. The oil temperature will drop when the chicken is added, so you may need to adjust the heat intermittently to maintain the oil temperature. Transfer to the paper towel-lined plate.

Serve the hot chicken with fresh coriander and the spicy mandarin sauce.

Kūmara & black bean enchiladas with pecan mole

hands-on time	1 hour
total time	1 hour 45 mins
serves	4–6 as a main

(VE)

Traditional mole uses ancho chillies, which give a signature smoky flavour to the sauce. These are found at most specialty food stores, but if unavailable, you can use any mild dried chilli. The deep brown colour of the enchiladas is thanks to the ancho chillies and dark chocolate in the delicious mole. Best made with Sunset wraps (page 230) or you can use store-bought medium–large flour tortillas.

Preheat the oven to 180°C fan-forced (or 200°C conventional). Line a large oven tray with baking paper.

First prepare the enchilada filling. In a large bowl, toss the kūmara, capsicum and red onion with the olive oil, paprika, coriander, cumin and salt. Place in a single layer on the oven tray and roast for 20–25 minutes, until the kūmara is just cooked through (a knife should go through easily, but you do not want it to be too soft). Return the roasted vegetables to the bowl and add the black beans, spinach, coriander, lime zest and juice. Toss together, adjust seasoning to taste and set aside.

Reduce the oven temperature to 160°C fan-forced (or 180°C conventional).

Next make the pecan mole. In a large frying pan over medium heat, toast the dried ancho chillies for a couple of minutes until starting to soften and become fragrant. Transfer the chillies to a bowl, cover with boiling water, and set aside for 20 minutes to rehydrate. Meanwhile, return the frying pan to the heat. Add the pecans and sultanas and toast for a couple of minutes, until fragrant and starting to brown a little. Add the sesame seeds and toast for a further minute until all are golden brown. Transfer to a blender (or food processor). Heat the olive oil in the pan and add the onion. Sauté for 8 minutes until softened. Add the chopped chilli and garlic and cook for 2 minutes, tossing through the onions. Add the spices and oregano and fry for a further minute. Transfer to the blender. Drain the ancho chillies and add to the blender with the tomato paste, balsamic and 250ml stock. Blitz to a smooth sauce.

Pour the sauce into a medium–large saucepan. Add the remaining 500ml stock and bring to the boil over high heat, then reduce the heat to medium and simmer for 10 minutes to reduce a little. Add the chocolate, tahini, maple syrup, salt and pepper, stirring through until the chocolate has melted into the sauce. Simmer for a few extra minutes, to make a slightly thickened, pourable sauce. Adjust seasoning to taste and remove from the heat.

Enchilada filling

2 orange kūmara (about 750g total), peeled and cut into 2cm chunks

1 medium yellow or red capsicum, cored, deseeded and thinly sliced

1 red onion, thinly sliced

2 tbsp olive oil

1 tsp ground paprika

1 tsp ground coriander

1 tsp ground cumin

1 tsp sea salt

400g can black beans, rinsed and drained

75g baby spinach leaves

2 tbsp chopped coriander leaves

finely grated zest and freshly squeezed juice of 1 lime

Pecan mole

4 dried ancho chillies, stems removed

70g pecans, roughly chopped

40g sultanas

1 tbsp sesame seeds

2 tbsp olive oil

1 red onion, finely chopped

1 long red chilli, finely chopped

4 cloves garlic, finely chopped

2 tsp ground cumin

1 tsp ground cinnamon

½ tsp ground star anise

1 tsp dried oregano

1 tbsp tomato paste

1 tbsp balsamic vinegar

750ml vegetable stock

50g vegan dark chocolate, finely chopped

1 tbsp tahini

1 tbsp maple syrup

1 tsp sea salt

½ tsp cracked black pepper

Additional ingredients

8 sunset wraps (page 230), or medium–large flour tortillas

flesh of 2 avocados, sliced

2 spring onions, thinly sliced

1 green chilli, finely chopped

1 handful coriander leaves

juice of 1 lime

To assemble the enchiladas, spoon a thin layer of the pecan mole into the base of a large baking dish. Take one tortilla and spoon 3 tbsp of the filling down the centre. Roll tightly to enclose and place in the baking dish, seam-side down. Repeat with the remaining tortillas and filling, so that they fit snugly in a single layer in the base of the baking dish. Pour the remaining mole sauce evenly over the rolled tortillas to cover, and bake for 25 minutes, until bubbling.

To serve, toss the avocado, spring onion, green chilli, coriander and lime juice together. Scatter over the top of the baked enchiladas and serve warm.

hands-on time	45 mins
total time	3 hours
(+ overnight marinating)	
serves	6–8

Harissa roast lamb with minted pomegranate gravy

2.5kg lamb leg, bone-in

1 tbsp rose harissa (page 217)

280g unsweetened natural Greek yoghurt, plus extra for serving

6 cloves garlic, peeled

freshly squeezed juice of 1 lemon

3 tbsp chopped almonds

2 tbsp soft brown sugar

1 tsp black peppercorns

½ tsp sea salt

handful mint leaves, to serve

pomegranate seeds, to serve

Minted pomegranate gravy

375ml vegetable stock

60ml pomegranate molasses

½ tsp dried mint

roast lamb juices (about 250ml)

3 tbsp plain flour

The secret to this lamb is in the harrisa yoghurt marinade – best prepared the night before. The gravy is seriously addictive, with pomegranate complementing the classic combo of mint and lamb. It's the perfect celebration centrepiece.

Marinate the lamb in advance. Place the lamb leg fat-side up in a flameproof roasting dish large enough for it to sit flat. Pat dry with paper towel. Using a sharp knife, score the meat with a series of shallow cuts a couple of centimetres apart (this will allow the marinade to penetrate the meat). For the marinade, place the rose harissa, yoghurt, garlic, lemon juice, almonds, brown sugar, peppercorns and salt in a blender (or food processor). Blitz on high until relatively smooth. Pour the marinade over the lamb leg. Using your hands, massage the marinade into the lamb. Cover with clingfilm and refrigerate overnight (or at least 5 hours). Remove the lamb from the fridge 1 hour before you start cooking.

Preheat the oven to 160°C fan-forced (or 180°C conventional).

To roast the lamb, pour 250ml water into the base of the roasting dish (do not pour over the lamb). Tent the roasting dish with foil with the shiny side facing inwards and sealing tightly. Roast the lamb for 1 hour 30 minutes.

Remove the foil and return the lamb to the oven for a further 40 minutes, basting every 15 minutes with the juices in the roasting dish. If you like, at the end of roasting time, change the oven function to grill and grill for a few minutes to brown the top of the lamb further. Transfer the lamb to a serving platter, cover with foil and leave to rest for 20 minutes. Reserve the liquid (should be about 250ml) in the roasting dish for the gravy.

For the minted pomegranate gravy, place the vegetable stock, pomegranate molasses and dried mint in a saucepan over medium heat. Bring to the boil then reduce the heat to low to keep warm. Place the roasting dish containing the meat juices on the stove top over medium heat (or pour into a frying pan). When the juices are bubbling, sprinkle over the flour and stir for a couple of minutes to cook the flour a little, scraping all the caramelised meat juices from the bottom as you go. Stirring continuously, pour the warmed stock mixture a little at a time into the roasting dish. Simmer for 10 minutes, until nicely thickened. Strain through a sieve before pouring into a jug to serve.

Serve the roast lamb topped with a few dollops of extra yoghurt, finely chopped mint, whole mint leaves and pomegranate seeds, with the gravy on the side.

Paneer & shiitake biryani with saffron-rose milk

hands-on time	1 hour 10 mins
total time	2 hours
serves	4–6 as a main

(GF)

Shiitake mushrooms give a buttery umami flavour, but portobello or oyster mushrooms will also do well. Serve with your favourite raita – I like to simply mix yoghurt, mint and lemon juice together.

First marinate the paneer. Place the paneer, yoghurt, turmeric, cumin, lemon zest, juice, herbs and 1 tsp salt in a bowl. Toss together to coat the paneer evenly. Cover and refrigerate for 1 hour.

To prepare the rice, place the rice in a sieve and rinse under cold running water until the water draining from the rice runs clear. Drain well. Place into a bowl, cover with cold water and set aside to soak for 30 minutes.

Preheat the oven to 180°C fan-forced (or 200°C conventional).

For the paneer & shiitake, heat 4 tbsp of the canola oil in a 24cm Dutch oven or large heavy-based saucepan over medium heat. Add the onion and cook for 20 minutes, stirring occasionally, until deeply caramelised. Remove two-thirds of the onion and set aside to sprinkle over the biryani layers. Add another 1 tbsp canola oil to the onion in the pan, then add the garlic, ginger, cardamom pods, cloves, fennel and cumin seeds and cook, stirring, for 1 minute. Add the mushrooms, green beans, garam masala, ground chilli, cinnamon, pepper and remaining 1 tsp salt. Cook for 5 minutes, stirring occasionally, until the mushrooms are soft and beans are starting to brown. Finally, add the paneer and its yoghurt marinade and cook over medium heat for 5 minutes – you should be left with a fairly thick sauce. Transfer half of the paneer mixture to a separate bowl and leave the other half in the base of the Dutch oven (if you used a saucepan, transfer half the mixture to a 24cm casserole dish with a lid). Set aside.

To prepare the saffron-rose milk, in a small saucepan over medium heat, heat the milk until just starting to steam and the odd bubble appears (you do not want to boil the milk). Remove from the heat, add the rose water and sprinkle over the saffron strands. Set aside for 15 minutes.

To partially cook the rice, drain the rice and place into a medium–large saucepan. Add 1 litre of cold water, the lemon zest, juice, cardamom pods, bay leaves, cinnamon stick and salt. Bring to the boil over high heat and cook for 3 minutes, until partially cooked (if you break open a grain of rice you should see a clear outer ring with a harder white core). Drain well and discard the whole spices. Set aside.

Paneer & shiitake

500g paneer, cut into 2cm cubes
280g unsweetened natural yoghurt
1 tsp ground turmeric
1 tsp ground cumin
finely grated zest and freshly squeezed juice of ½ lemon
2 tbsp chopped coriander
2 tbsp chopped mint leaves
2 tsp sea salt
5 tbsp canola oil
3 red onions, thinly sliced
6 cloves garlic, finely chopped
1 tbsp finely grated fresh ginger
4 green cardamom pods
4 cloves
½ tsp fennel seeds
½ tsp cumin seeds
250g shiitake mushrooms, stalks removed, cut into 1cm thick slices
250g green beans, ends trimmed, cut into 5cm pieces
1 tsp garam masala
1 tsp ground chilli
½ tsp ground cinnamon
½ tsp cracked black pepper

Saffron-rose milk

60ml milk
2 tsp rose water
1 large pinch (about 25 strands) of saffron threads

Rice

400g basmati rice

finely grated zest and freshly
squeezed juice of ½ lemon

4 green cardamom pods

2 bay leaves

1 cinnamon stick

1 tsp sea salt

Biryani assembly

1 tbsp canola oil

35g cashews

40g sultanas

½ green chilli, finely chopped

1 tbsp chopped coriander, extra

1 tbsp chopped mint, extra

To assemble the biryani, heat 1 tbsp canola oil in a small frying pan over medium heat. Cook the cashews for a couple of minutes until starting to turn golden. Add the sultanas and cook for a further 30 seconds. Transfer to a bowl.

Spoon half the partially cooked rice over the paneer mixture in the Dutch oven. Sprinkle with half the caramelised onions, half the saffron-rose milk, the green chilli and the extra coriander and mint. Spoon the remaining paneer mixture evenly on top, cover with the remaining rice, onion and saffron-rose milk. Sprinkle with the cashews and sultanas. Cover tightly with two pieces of foil then place the lid on top. Bake for 25 minutes. Remove from the oven and leave to stand for 10 minutes. Uncover, remove the foil and loosen the rice a little with a fork.

Serve immediately, with your favourite raita.

Delight

Baking & desserts

The sweeter things have been prominent in my life; deliciousness in moments of triumph and disaster, formality and hilarity. It was my search for the ultimate chocolate chip cookie that led me to some of my best memories exploring the back blocks of New York City. Then there was the time I baked seriously red-faced brownies following the accidental death of the neighbour's cat. Or the Summer's day baby shower where we had three people holding a melting cake under an air-conditioning unit as I iced my ass off. What I've come to realise is that my connection to the sweet stuff was inevitable. I look to my whānau, and see that baking and desserts are ingrained in our DNA.

My mum has undoubtedly been my biggest baking influence. Thinking back to the food she made while working full time, food that I often took for granted, it was absolute kitchen wizardry. Freshly baked lemon and poppy seed muffins, fragrant and fluffy with their crunchy lemony sugar topping. The infamous sculpted chocolate chip biscuit birthday cakes. Her crème de la crème hazelnut torte, layers of chewy hazelnut meringue sandwiched with oozing boysenberries, hardened chocolate, and pillowy cream. Pure magic. She inspired me then and she inspires me now.

When we lived in Oamaru, our backyard was home to a grand old cooking apple tree. By autumn's arrival the tree would be heaving with green globes, in such quantities that many would drop and attract droves of Monarch butterflies to feast on the fallen fruit. Seeing it go to waste, my dad decided to take it upon himself to make the most of the tree's generous offerings. And so the era of Dad's apple pies began. Heavenly smells of fruit and pastry filled the kitchen and deep into my memory. When I think of apple pie, I think of him.

It's not just my parents. Memories of my grandparents are filled with moments of sweetness. Like Grandma Peg's shortbread or Grandma Maureen's biscuit tin, which played host to a game of biscuit roulette; if you were lucky, a dreamy chocolate biscuit or a slice of her famous fruitcake. Or would it be the turn of the dreaded salty 'Lemon Treats'?

Delight is as much about the pleasure in the process as it is about the treats themselves. Baking and desserts are a universal love language, a way for us to share ourselves, and often our family history with others.

This chapter is filled with recipes where through a little bit of science and a whole lotta magic, simple ingredients are transformed into something truly special. So if you're looking for your classic banana cake, I'm afraid you'll be sorely disappointed. Some of these recipes take inspiration from traditionally savoury botanicals that I've found complement sweetness equally well, such as the Dark chocolate, basil & banana cake with basil ganache & crystallised basil leaves (page 184) or Saffron yoghurt panna cotta with honey-mint oranges & almond crumble (page 186). Others give a welcome twist to the slightly more familiar, like the Grapefruit & thyme meringue pie (page 196) and Peanut masala caramel slice (page 200). There are also some winning vegan delights found in these pages too – the Chai, date & banana self-saucing pudding with tahini cream (page 204) is not to be missed.

I hope that these recipes are an adventure and bring to your home the wonder and joy that they bring to mine. Don't forget to lick the spoon.

Roasted thyme peaches with cardamom ginger ice cream & rum caramel

hands-on time	30 mins
total time	45 mins
	(+ overnight freezing)
serves	6

Don't be thrown by the fact that you're making your own ice cream here – it's a no-churn recipe that is fail-safe. Make the cardamom ginger ice cream a day ahead, and the rum-spiked caramel sauce can be made in advance, too. Use the freshest, juiciest peaches you can find.

Make the cardamom ginger ice cream a day ahead. Pour the cream and condensed milk into a large bowl, and using an electric hand or stand mixer, beat on high until thick and forming medium-stiff peaks when the mixer whisk attachment is lifted out. Gently fold in the cardamom and ginger. Spoon into a standard loaf tin (about 24cm x 12cm) and smooth the surface with the back of a spoon. Cover loosely with clingfilm and place in the freezer overnight (for a minimum of 8 hours).

For the rum caramel, combine the sugar and 60ml water in a deep saucepan over medium-low heat. Melt the sugar into the water until fully dissolved, then increase the heat to medium-high. Do NOT stir beyond this point. Bring to the boil and cook for 5–10 minutes, until the mixture is a deep amber colour. Remove from the heat and while stirring, carefully pour in the cream (stand back as it will bubble like a cauldron). Return to low heat and whisk until smooth. Add the butter, rum and salt, again whisking until smooth. Remove from the heat and using an electric hand mixer, beat the caramel on high for 3 minutes to emulsify the butter and create a smooth caramel. Pour into a jar and set aside to cool to room temperature.

Preheat the oven to 190°C fan-forced (or 210°C conventional). Line an oven tray with baking paper.

To cook the roasted thyme peaches, place the peach halves on the oven tray, cut side up. Sprinkle thyme over each peach half and drizzle with maple syrup. Roast for 20 minutes, until the peaches have softened but hold their shape and the edges are curled and golden brown. Remove the ice cream from the freezer 5 minutes before serving to soften it a little, ready for scooping.

Serve the roasted thyme peaches immediately, straight from the oven, with a large scoop of ice cream, a generous drizzle of rum caramel and a sprig of fresh thyme.

Cardamom ginger ice cream

500ml cream

395g can condensed milk

2 tsp ground cardamom

100g crystallised ginger, chopped into 5mm pieces

Rum caramel

200g caster sugar

85ml cream

75g butter, cubed

4 tbsp golden rum

1 tsp sea salt

Roasted thyme peaches

6 ripe yellow-flesh peaches, halved and pitted

1 tbsp thyme leaves, finely chopped, plus sprigs to serve

2 tbsp maple syrup

hands-on time	20 mins
total time	1 hour 30 mins
serves	12

Black sesame, rose & cardamom cake with honey mascarpone icing

Cake batter

100g butter, softened to room temperature

200g caster sugar

2 eggs

125ml canola oil

2 tbsp rose water

2 tsp vanilla extract

75g black tahini

125ml coconut cream

150g plain flour

110g ground almonds

2 tsp baking powder

1 tsp ground cardamom

¼ tsp sea salt

¼ tsp ground black pepper

To decorate

1 tbsp white sesame seeds

1 tbsp black sesame seeds

200g mascarpone

1 ½ tbsp honey, plus extra to drizzle

2 tsp rose water

If there is a quintessentially *me* cake, this is it. This cake has fed hungry hospital nurses, been cut by a married couple, and even featured as the base for one of my showstoppers on *The Great Kiwi Bake Off*. I love how visually striking the grey tones of the crumb are against the whipped cloud-like mascarpone. The combination of black sesame, rose, cardamom and black pepper is an unusual one, and it's sure to become a favourite.

Preheat the oven to 160°C fan-forced (or 180°C conventional). Grease a 20cm round cake tin and line with baking paper.

To make the cake, beat the butter and sugar in a large bowl, using an electric hand or stand mixer with the paddle attachment, for 3 minutes or until pale and fluffy. Add the eggs and beat for 1 minute, until well combined. Pour in the oil, rose water and vanilla. Beat for 1 minute, until smooth. Add the black tahini and coconut cream and beat for an additional minute, until smooth. In a separate bowl, whisk together the flour, ground almonds, baking powder, cardamom, salt and pepper. Fold the dry ingredients into the wet until smooth and just combined. There should be no remaining specks of flour left in the cake batter. Pour into the cake tin and bake for 45–50 minutes, or until a skewer inserted into the centre of the cake comes out clean. Leave to cool in the tin for 15 minutes before turning onto a wire rack to cool completely.

To decorate, toast the sesame seeds in a small frying pan over medium heat for a few minutes, until starting to brown and pop. Transfer to a small bowl to cool. In a separate bowl, whisk together the mascarpone, honey and rose water until smooth. Pipe or spread the honey mascarpone evenly over the top of the cooled cake, then sprinkle with the toasted seeds and drizzle with extra honey.

Serve on the day of baking, or refrigerate in an airtight container for up to 4 days. Bring to room temperature before serving.

Caramelised white chocolate, coconut & passionfruit crème brûlées

hands-on time	20 mins
total time	1 hour 10 mins (+ chilling time)
serves	6

(GF)

You can buy caramelised white chocolate from most supermarkets, but it is easily made (page 223) and delivers a deep, rich caramel undertone that pairs beautifully with the passionfruit and coconut.

Preheat the oven to 130°C fan-forced (or 150°C conventional). Place 6 ramekins (150–200ml each) in the base of a large baking dish.

Prepare the passionfruit for the crème brûlées. Scoop the passionfruit pulp into a sieve set over a bowl. Using the back of a spoon, press the passionfruit pulp to extract the juice – you'll need 60ml of juice. Transfer the seeds and pulp to a small dish and refrigerate until needed. Set the passionfruit juice aside.

To make the crème brûlées, whisk the egg yolks and sugar in a large bowl until pale and the sugar has dissolved. Place the chopped chocolate in a bowl. Heat the coconut cream and cream in a saucepan over medium heat until trembling and just starting to bubble. Pour the hot cream over the chocolate and whisk until the chocolate has melted completely. Slowly pour the chocolate cream into the egg mixture, whisking as you go, until smooth. Add the passionfruit juice and stir through. Gently strain through a sieve into a large jug or pouring bowl, being careful not to create too many bubbles. Pour boiling water into the baking dish around the ramekins, to come halfway up the sides. Carefully pour the brûlée mixture into the ramekins.

Bake for 45–50 minutes, until the custards are set but with a slight wobble in the centre. Remove from the oven, carefully lift the ramekins out of the water and place on a heatproof surface. Leave to cool completely at room temperature. Cover with clingfilm and refrigerate for at least 4 hours (or overnight) until completely set.

When nearly ready to serve, toast the coconut for a few minutes in a small frying pan over medium-high heat, stirring regularly, until golden brown. Transfer to a bowl and set aside to cool. Sprinkle 1 tsp caster sugar over each custard. Using a kitchen blowtorch, heat the sugar until caramelised and golden brown. Leave for a few minutes to cool and harden. Serve immediately, topped with a tsp of the reserved passionfruit seeds/pulp and a sprinkle of toasted coconut.

Note: If you don't have a kitchen blowtorch, preheat the oven grill to its hottest temperature. Sprinkle the sugar over the brûlées and place under the grill, with the oven door open, for a minute or so until the sugar starts to bubble and caramelise. Remove from the oven and leave to cool to allow the caramel to harden.

4–6 passionfruit (to make 60ml juice)

6 egg yolks

50g caster sugar

100g caramelised white chocolate, finely chopped (page 223)

400ml can full-fat coconut cream

125ml cream

To serve

4 tbsp thread coconut

6 tsp caster sugar

hands-on time	25 mins
total time	1 hour
makes	20 medium cookies

Salted chocolate, hazelnut & muscovado cookies

110g hazelnuts, roughly chopped

200g butter, softened to room temperature

100g caster sugar

100g muscovado sugar

100g soft brown sugar

1 egg

1 tsp vanilla extract

300g plain flour

¾ tsp bicarbonate of soda

¾ tsp baking powder

¾ tsp sea salt

250g milk chocolate, roughly chopped into 1–2cm chunks

sea salt flakes, to sprinkle

My ultimate cookie: soft and chewy, with deep caramel sugar flavour and loaded with big chunks of chocolate. Add roasted hazelnuts and a sprinkling of sea salt and you have a winner.

Preheat the oven to 160°C fan-forced (or 180°C conventional). Line 2 large oven trays with baking paper.

First roast the hazelnuts. Place the chopped hazelnuts in a single layer on one oven tray. Roast the hazelnuts for 12 minutes, until fragrant and golden brown. Set aside to cool to room temperature.

To make the cookie dough, beat the butter in a large bowl with an electric hand or stand mixer for 2 minutes, until starting to become pale and creamy. Add the sugars and beat for 2 minutes, until well combined and fluffy. Add the egg and vanilla and beat for a further minute, until combined. In a separate bowl, sift together the flour, bicarb soda, baking powder and salt. Using a wooden spoon, fold the dry ingredients into the wet and mix to form a soft dough. Add the hazelnuts and chocolate, stirring into the dough until evenly distributed. Roll the mixture into 20 balls (about 50–60g each, just bigger than a golf ball), ensuring a piece of chocolate is at the top of each, as this will give you pools of chocolate on your cookies. Place on a baking paper-lined tray (not the oven tray), ensuring they are not touching, and freeze for 15–20 minutes, until firm to the touch and chilled.

Arrange 6 balls of cookie dough onto each of the 2 lined oven trays, evenly spaced at least 5cm apart, as they will spread during baking. Bake for 15–20 minutes, swapping the trays halfway through, until golden brown and slightly cracked on top. Remove from the oven and sprinkle with sea salt flakes. If you want to 'scoot' your cookies to make them perfectly round, do so now (see note below). Leave to cool for 10 minutes then transfer to a wire rack to cool completely. Repeat with the remaining cookie dough balls, or you can leave these in the freezer in an airtight container for future cookies on demand. There is no need to thaw, just simply bake from frozen.

Note on 'scooting' cookies: As soon as they come out of the oven, take a round glass or cutter with an opening just larger than the cookies, place upside down to enclose the cookie (like capturing an insect) and, keeping contact with the oven tray, move the glass in a circle so that it nudges the uneven edges of the cookie inwards to form a perfect circle.

Dark chocolate, basil & banana cake with basil ganache & crystallised basil leaves

hands-on time	30 mins
total time	1 hour 30 mins (+ drying time for crystallised basil leaves)
serves	12

(VE)

I love the fudginess of this cake, thanks to the melted chocolate, banana and olive oil in the batter. The crystallised basil makes a stunning decoration with its simplicity, and I often make these the day before decorating, as they need a few hours to dry out and crystallise completely.

Preheat the oven to 160°C fan-forced (or 180°C conventional). Grease a 20cm round cake tin with oil and line with baking paper.

First make the crystallised basil leaves. In a small bowl, whisk the aquafaba until frothy. Place the caster sugar in a separate shallow bowl. Take one basil leaf, dip in the aquafaba to coat then brush each side of the leaf against the edge of the bowl to remove any excess. Hold the leaf over the bowl of sugar and use a teaspoon to sprinkle sugar over each side of the basil leaf to coat. Shake off any excess. Transfer to a paper towel-lined plate and repeat with the remaining leaves. Set aside, uncovered, to dry for about 2 hours, or overnight.

To make the cake, place the chocolate and milk in a heatproof bowl over a saucepan one-third full with simmering water. Gently whisk until the chocolate has melted completely into the milk. Stir in the coffee granules and remove from the heat. In a large bowl, whisk together the banana, olive oil, sugars and vanilla until well combined. Pour in the melted chocolate mixture and whisk until smooth. In a separate bowl, sift together the flour, ground almonds, cocoa, baking powder, cinnamon and salt. Fold the dry ingredients into the wet and gently mix to form a smooth batter (there should be no remaining specks of flour). Finally, fold in the chopped basil. Pour the cake batter into the cake tin and bake for 45–50 minutes, until a skewer inserted into the centre of the cake comes out reasonably clean. Leave to cool in the tin for 15 minutes before turning onto a wire rack to cool.

For the basil ganache, place the chocolate in a wide bowl (make sure the chocolate is finely chopped so you don't end up with a lumpy ganache). Heat the coconut cream and basil leaves in a small saucepan over medium heat until the cream is just starting to bubble at the edges. Pour the hot cream through a sieve over the chocolate, pressing the basil leaves to release as much of the basil flavour as possible. Discard the leaves. Tilt the bowl to ensure all the chocolate is submerged in the cream, and leave for 2 minutes for the cream to melt the chocolate. Stir to make a smooth, glossy ganache. Set aside to cool to a thick but spreadable consistency.

Crystallised basil leaves

40g aquafaba (liquid drained from canned chickpeas)

100g caster sugar

16 basil leaves

Cake batter

150g vegan dark chocolate, roughly chopped

250ml milk (almond, oat or coconut)

1 tbsp instant coffee granules

2 ripe bananas, mashed with a fork

125ml olive oil

100g caster sugar

100g soft brown sugar

2 tsp vanilla extract

150g plain flour

110g ground almonds

50g cocoa powder

1 tsp baking powder

¾ tsp ground cinnamon

½ tsp sea salt

4 tbsp (about 20g) finely chopped basil leaves

Basil ganache

200g vegan dark chocolate, finely chopped

200ml coconut cream

20 basil leaves

To ice and decorate the cake, spoon the basil ganache onto the centre of the cake. Using the back of a spoon, spread the ganache evenly over the top of the cake. Leave the ganache to set (you can refrigerate the cake to speed this up) then top with the crystallised basil leaves.

To serve, cut into slices. Keep any leftovers in an airtight container at room temperature for up to 3 days.

Saffron yoghurt panna cotta with honey-mint oranges & almond crumble

hands-on time	30 mins
total time	45 mins (+ chilling time)
serves	6

Saffron is not only brilliant in savoury cooking; its floral taste and aroma lends itself equally well to the sweeter side. This is an excellent make-ahead dessert to impress guests – all three components can be prepared in advance, if desired.

Lightly grease 6 dariole moulds or ramekins (about 150–200ml) with a little canola oil to coat the base and sides. Place the moulds onto a board.

For the panna cotta, place 85ml of the cream in a small bowl and sprinkle over the gelatine. Stir to combine and set aside to allow the gelatine to bloom. Combine the remaining 500ml cream with the orange zest, saffron threads and sugar in a saucepan. Heat over medium-low heat, stirring until the sugar is dissolved, then increase to medium-high heat. When just starting to boil, immediately remove from the heat. Whisk in the gelatine mixture until the gelatine is completely dissolved then leave for 2 minutes to cool slightly. Place the yoghurt in a large pouring bowl or jug and whisk until smooth. Strain the heated cream through a sieve into the bowl with the yoghurt, pouring slowly to avoid forming too many bubbles. Press the orange zest and saffron to release any remaining liquid. Gently whisk the mixture until smooth then carefully pour into the moulds to fill just below the rim. Cover with clingfilm, ensuring it doesn't touch the liquid. Place in the refrigerator for a minimum of 4 hours (or overnight) to set. These can be made up to 3 days in advance.

Prepare the honey-mint oranges at least 1 hour before serving. Warm the honey in a small saucepan over low heat until the honey is runny and liquid. Place the orange segments and mint in a bowl and pour over the warm honey. Toss to coat then set aside for at least 1 hour, for the flavours to amalgamate.

Preheat the oven to 160°C fan-forced (or 180°C conventional). Line an oven tray with baking paper.

To make the almond crumble, place the ground almonds, flour, sugar and salt in a bowl and whisk together with a fork. Rub the butter into the dry ingredients until starting to resemble breadcrumbs. Stir through the chopped almonds and spread onto the oven tray. Bake for 12–15 minutes, until golden brown. Leave to cool to room temperature before breaking up into a crumble.

Panna cotta

canola oil, to grease

585ml cream

10g powdered gelatine

finely grated zest of 1 orange

¼ tsp saffron threads

100g caster sugar

280g unsweetened natural Greek yoghurt

Honey-mint oranges

2 tbsp honey

2 oranges, peeled and cut into segments

10 mint leaves, thinly sliced

Almond crumble

55g ground almonds

50g plain flour

50g soft brown sugar

¼ tsp sea salt

50g chilled butter, cut into small cubes

45g almonds, roughly chopped

When ready to serve, remove the clingfilm from the panna cotta. Dip each mould into a bowl of hot water for 10–30 seconds (depending on the thickness of the mould or ramekin), ensuring no water gets on the panna cotta. Run the blunt tip of a small butter knife around the top edge of the mould to separate the panna cotta a little. Place a plate on top of each panna cotta and invert the mould onto the plate. Give it a reasonable tap or shake and the panna cotta should come out (if not, it may need a few more seconds in the hot water to loosen). Sprinkle the almond crumble around the base of each panna cotta and serve with the honey-mint oranges and a spoonful of the syrup. Serve immediately.

Spiced pear & chocolate croissant pudding with pistachios & orange

hands-on time	40 mins
total time	1 hour 15 mins
serves	6

This recipe is the next level version of the classic bread-and-butter pudding, using torn croissants to soak up the neatly spiced orange custard, then layered with caramelised pears, chocolate, and pistachios.

Preheat the oven to 170°C fan-forced (or 190°C conventional). Grease the base and sides of a round baking dish (about 25cm diameter) generously with butter.

First infuse the cream. Place 375ml of the cream, caster sugar, orange peel, orange juice, cinnamon stick, star anise and ginger in a saucepan over medium-high heat. Heat the mixture, stirring to dissolve the sugar, until it is just starting to bubble. Remove from the heat and leave to stand for 30 minutes, to allow the flavours to infuse into the cream.

To caramelise the pears, heat a frying pan over medium heat. Add the pears, butter, brown sugar, cinnamon and ginger and cook for 5 minutes, until the pears are softened and starting to caramelise. Remove from the heat and set aside to cool for 10 minutes.

To finish the custard, strain the infused cream through a sieve into a bowl or jug. Crack the eggs into the cream and whisk until well combined.

To assemble, place the torn croissant pieces and chopped dark chocolate into the baking dish, tossing together. Layer the caramelised pears among the croissants, drizzle with the pear cooking liquid, then evenly pour the custard over. Bake for 25–30 minutes, until the custard is set and the croissants are puffed up and golden. Set aside to cool for 5 minutes.

To serve, place the remaining 125ml cream in a small bowl and using an electric hand mixer, beat the cream to form soft peaks. Scatter the chopped pistachios over the pudding and serve warm with the whipped cream.

500ml cream

50g caster sugar

peeled zest of 1 orange

60ml freshly squeezed orange juice

1 cinnamon stick

1 star anise

1 thumb-sized piece of ginger, peeled and sliced

2 Beurre Bosc pears, halved, cored and thinly sliced

30g butter

2 tbsp soft brown sugar

1 tsp ground cinnamon

1 tsp ground ginger

4 eggs

4 large croissants, torn into 3cm pieces

100g dark chocolate, roughly chopped

50g pistachio kernels, roasted and roughly chopped

hands-on time	15 mins
total time	45 mins (+ chilling time)
makes	1 large rectangular tin

Tahini, white chocolate & boysenberry brownie

400g butter, cut into small cubes

250g dark chocolate, roughly chopped

6 eggs

1 tbsp vanilla extract

400g caster sugar

130g soft brown sugar

335g plain flour

100g cocoa powder

1 tsp baking powder

½ tsp sea salt

200g white chocolate, roughly chopped

4 tbsp tahini

150g frozen boysenberries, halved

This brownie is the ultimate in fudgy deliciousness. You can substitute the boysenberries with frozen raspberries or blackberries, or use your favourite nut butter in place of tahini.

Preheat the oven to 160°C fan-forced (or 180°C conventional). Grease a large rectangular baking tin (about 33cm x 23cm) and line with baking paper.

To make the brownies, place the butter and dark chocolate in a heatproof bowl over a saucepan one-third full with simmering water. Gently whisk the butter and chocolate together until melted and smooth. Remove from the heat. In a large bowl with an electric hand mixer, beat the eggs, vanilla and sugars for 3 minutes, until it becomes pale and creamy. Pour in the melted butter and chocolate mixture and stir until smooth. In a separate bowl, sift together the flour, cocoa powder, baking powder and salt. Fold the dry ingredients into the wet until well combined and no specks of flour remain. Stir in the chopped white chocolate and pour into the prepared baking tin, spreading out with a spatula to evenly fill the tin.

Dollop the tahini on top of the batter and using a teaspoon, drag the tahini out to create a swirling effect. Dot the boysenberry halves between the swirls of tahini and lightly press into the batter (they should still be seen above the surface). Bake for 25–30 minutes, or until the brownie is cooked on top but the centre still wobbles a little when the tin is moved. Leave to cool to room temperature then refrigerate for at least 3 hours, until completely set, before cutting. Store in an airtight container in the refrigerator for up to 5 days.

Quick-fried pineapple with spiced mango custard & minted lime sugar

hands-on time	40 mins
total time	40 mins
serves	8

I love caramelised pineapple, and this is one of my favourite ways to serve it. The custard is reminiscent of a thick mango lassi, and is equally good on its own or stuffed into brioche doughnuts. I use amchur in the lime sugar for its sour notes, but the dish is still worth making without it.

First make the spiced mango custard. In a blender or food processor, blitz the mango flesh until relatively smooth then add the milk and blitz together until smooth (the milk will froth up a little). Transfer to a saucepan and bring slowly to the boil over medium heat. Place the remaining custard ingredients in a large bowl and whisk together. Once the mango milk is just starting to bubble, remove from the heat and strain through a fine sieve into a separate bowl, stirring and pushing the mango milk through the sieve with the back of a spoon. Discard any leftover mango pulp. Gradually pour the hot mango milk into the egg mixture, whisking together until relatively smooth, then pour the mixture back into a clean saucepan. Return to medium heat and whisk until the mixture is bubbling and thickened. Remove from the heat and transfer to a bowl. Cover the surface of the custard with clingfilm to prevent a skin forming, and set aside to cool to room temperature.

To prepare the minted lime sugar, use a mortar and pestle to pound mint, sugar, amchur and lime zest in a circular motion, until the mint disintegrates and combines with the sugar. Set aside.

For the quick-fried pineapple, cut off the top and bottom, then stand upright and cut off the skin from top to bottom, following the shape of the pineapple. Cut into quarters lengthways and remove the core from each quarter. Cut each quarter lengthways into four to make 16 long wedges. Melt the butter in a large frying pan over medium heat. Add the sugar and pineapple wedges and cook for a couple of minutes on each side, turning to coat in the butter until golden brown and caramelised. Add the lime juice and cardamom, toss through the pineapple for a minute, then remove from the heat.

To serve, spoon the spiced mango custard into bowls, top with 2 slices of the warm caramelised pineapple and dot the minted lime sugar over the fruit. Add a couple of small mint leaves for garnish.

Spiced mango custard

300g mango flesh (from 2 ripe mangoes)

375ml full-fat milk

4 egg yolks

65g caster sugar

20g cornflour

10g plain flour

½ tsp ground turmeric

½ tsp ground cardamom

½ tsp ground cinnamon

1 tbsp honey

Minted lime sugar

20 mint leaves, plus extra to serve

3 tbsp caster sugar

1 tsp amchur

finely grated zest of 1 lime

Quick-fried pineapple

1 large ripe pineapple

40g butter

1 tbsp muscovado sugar

freshly squeezed juice of 1 lime

¼ tsp ground cardamom

Pistachio, lime & raspberry cake

|---|---|
hands-on time	40 mins
total time	1 hour 30 mins
makes	1 large rectangular cake

Cake batter

150g pistachio kernels

300g plain flour

300g caster sugar

1 ½ tsp baking powder

1 ½ tsp bicarbonate of soda

¼ tsp sea salt

200g sour cream

125ml canola oil

3 eggs

finely grated zest and freshly squeezed juice of 3 limes

150g frozen raspberries

Raspberry Swiss meringue buttercream

75g fresh or frozen raspberries

100g egg whites (about 3)

150g caster sugar

250g butter, at room temperature, cut into 3cm cubes

To decorate

pistachio kernels, roasted and roughly chopped

finely grated lime zest

This is the king of all party cakes. It's easy, looks spectacular, appeals to young and old, and is moist and flavour-packed. Swiss meringue buttercream is always worth the effort.

Preheat the oven to 160°C fan-forced (or 180°C conventional). Grease a large rectangular baking tin (about 33cm x 23cm) and line with baking paper.

To make the cake, place the pistachios in a food processor and blitz until finely ground. Transfer to a large bowl. Add the flour, sugar, baking powder, bicarb soda and salt, and whisk until evenly combined. Make a well in the centre and add the sour cream, oil, eggs, lime zest and juice. Whisk until well combined and smooth. Carefully pour 250ml boiling water into the batter and whisk until smooth. Pour into the prepared tin and sprinkle over the frozen raspberries.

Bake for 40 minutes, or until a skewer inserted into the centre of the cake comes out clean. Place on a wire rack and leave the cake to cool in the tin for 15 minutes. Run a knife around the edge of the cake to loosen. Carefully invert the cake onto a chopping board and peel off the baking paper. Cool fully then invert onto a serving board.

For the raspberry Swiss meringue buttercream, place the raspberries in a saucepan over medium heat. Cook for 3–5 minutes, mashing with a spoon, until the raspberries form a mushy purée. Pour into a bowl and set aside to cool completely. Place the egg whites and caster sugar in a clean large stand mixer bowl. Set over a saucepan one-third full with simmering water, ensuring the water is not touching the base of the bowl. Gently heat the egg whites and sugar, whisking with a wire whisk occasionally, until the egg whites are very warm and the sugar has dissolved (test this by dipping your thumb and forefinger into the egg white and rubbing them together – you shouldn't feel any grains of sugar). Transfer the bowl to the stand mixer fitted with the whisk attachment. Whisk on high speed for 5–7 minutes, until the meringue is stiff and the mixing bowl has cooled to room temperature. While continuing to whisk on high, add the butter one cube at a time, mixing to combine after each addition. The mixture will curdle partway through the mixing process – just keep adding the butter and it will become smooth. Gently mix the raspberry purée into the buttercream until combined.

To serve, spread the buttercream over the cooled cake and sprinkle generously with the pistachios and lime zest. Slice and serve immediately. Store any leftovers in an airtight container at room temperature for up to 3 days.

Grapefruit & thyme meringue pie

hands-on time	1 hour 15 mins
total time	2 hours 15 mins (+ chilling time)
serves	12

Rather than baking the pie in its entirety, this recipe only requires you to bake the pastry shell. The filling is then cooked on the stovetop, refrigerated until set, and topped with torched Swiss meringue. If you don't own a kitchen blowtorch, place the pie in the oven under the grill to brown the meringue a little before serving.

Preheat the oven to 160°C fan-forced (or 180°C conventional). Grease a 23–25cm fluted tart tin (with a removable base) with butter.

Line the tart tin. Place the chilled pastry dough on a lightly floured surface. Using a floured rolling pin, roll out into a large circle, big enough to cover the base and sides of the tin. Loosely roll up the pastry around the rolling pin, then unroll to drape the pastry over the tin and press into the base and sides. Trim off any excess pastry overhanging the edge and use this to fill in any holes or cracks. Place in the freezer for 20 minutes to rest and chill.

To blind bake the tart shell, prick the pastry base in a few places with a fork. Scrunch up a piece of baking paper big enough to line the pastry base and sides, then unscrunch, line the tart shell to cover the pastry, and fill with uncooked rice (or baking beads). Bake for 20 minutes. Remove the rice and baking paper, return the tart shell to the oven and bake for 5–10 minutes, until golden brown. Remove from the oven and leave to cool to room temperature.

For the grapefruit & thyme filling, place the grapefruit and lemon zest and juice and thyme in a saucepan over medium-high heat. Bring to the boil then reduce the heat to medium and simmer for 10 minutes. Strain and set the thyme-infused juice aside to cool a little – you should have around 250ml of juice. Add some water to the juice to make a total liquid volume of 375ml. In a saucepan, whisk together the egg yolks, sugar, honey and cornflour until smooth. Add the 375ml liquid and whisk until smooth. Place over medium-low heat and cook for a few minutes, whisking constantly, until very thick and bubbling. Remove from the heat and whisk in the butter until smooth and glossy. Pour immediately into the prepared tart shell and place clingfilm directly on the filling to cover. Refrigerate for at least 4 hours to chill until set, or up to 2 days if making ahead.

For the Swiss meringue, on the day of serving, place the egg whites and caster sugar in a stand mixer bowl. Set over a saucepan one-third full with simmering water, ensuring the water is not touching the base of the bowl. Gently whisk the egg whites and sugar with a wire whisk until the egg whites are warm and the sugar has dissolved (test this by dipping your thumb and forefinger into the egg white and rubbing

1 quantity Ginger sweet shortcrust pastry, chilled (page 222)

Grapefruit & thyme filling

finely grated zest of 4 grapefruits

finely grated zest of 1 lemon

400ml freshly squeezed grapefruit juice

50ml freshly squeezed lemon juice

10g thyme sprigs, plus extra to decorate

6 egg yolks

150g caster sugar

90g honey

50g cornflour

100g butter, chopped into small cubes

Swiss meringue

130g egg whites (about 4)

200g caster sugar

them together – you shouldn't feel any grains of sugar). Transfer the bowl back to the stand mixer fitted with a whisk attachment. Whisk on high speed for 5–7 minutes, until the meringue is stiff and the mixing bowl has cooled to room temperature.

To finish, cover the tart filling with the meringue (using a piping bag or a spoon to create peaks). Use a kitchen blowtorch to lightly toast the meringue until golden brown. Scatter a handful of thyme leaves over the meringue. Slice and serve. Store any leftovers in an airtight container in the refrigerator for up to 3 days.

hands-on time	35 mins
total time	45 mins
serves	12

(VE°) (S) (A)

Fig baklava nests with orange blossom syrup

75g walnuts

75g pistachio kernels

1 tbsp soft brown sugar

¾ tsp ground cardamom

½ tsp ground cinnamon

finely grated zest of ½ lemon

90ml olive oil

12 small fresh figs

6 large sheets vegan filo pastry (about 40cm x 30cm)

unsweetened natural Greek yoghurt (coconut if vegan), to serve

Orange blossom syrup

65g caster sugar

1 tbsp honey (maple syrup if vegan)

1 tbsp orange blossom water

freshly squeezed juice of ½ lemon

This recipe gives you all the baklava feels but turns tradition on its head – individual mini baklavas stuffed with juicy fresh figs and served warm, bathing in their orange blossom syrup.

Preheat the oven to 160°C fan-forced (or 180°C conventional). Grease a regular 12-hole muffin tin lightly with olive oil. Line an oven tray with baking paper.

For the baklava filling, place the walnuts and pistachios in a single layer on the oven tray. Bake for 8 minutes, until lightly roasted. Set aside to cool slightly. Place the nuts in a food processor and pulse a couple of times until finely chopped (or you can finely chop by hand). Transfer to a bowl and add the brown sugar, cardamom, cinnamon, lemon zest and 30ml of the olive oil. Mix together until well combined.

To prepare the figs, remove any stems, sit the figs upright and slice a cross into the top of each fig, cutting three-quarters of the way down so that they are quartered with the bottoms remaining intact.

To make the nests, lay 1 sheet of filo pastry on a board. Using the remaining 60ml of olive oil, brush the pastry with a little oil then carefully layer another sheet on top. Repeat, brushing each layer of pastry with a little oil until you have layered 6 sheets of pastry. Cut the pastry into twelve 10cm squares. Place into the muffin holes, pressing gently into the base and sides to form ruffled nests. Place one fig into each of the nests, standing upright. Spoon some of the baklava filling into the centre of each fig, spreading the quarters a little, and fill the pastry nests around the figs with the remaining filling. Bake for 15–20 minutes, until the pastry is golden brown.

Make the orange blossom syrup as the fig baklava nests bake. Stir the caster sugar, honey, orange blossom water, lemon juice and 60ml water in a small saucepan over medium heat until the sugar has dissolved. Increase the heat to medium-high, bring to the boil and then lower the heat slightly to rapid simmer, uncovered, for 5 minutes until reduced and thickened slightly. Set aside.

Remove the baklava nests from the oven and while still hot, drizzle with a little of the orange blossom syrup. Leave in the tins for 10 minutes to cool a little and allow the syrup to soak in. Remove from the tins and serve warm with a pool of yoghurt and a drizzle of any remaining syrup.

Peanut masala caramel slice

hands-on time	30 mins
total time	1 hour (+ cooling and chilling time)
makes	1 large rectangular tin

Nothing quite measures up to the absolute caramel slice ecstasy that is achieved from a condensed milk caramel layer. Garam masala gives the caramel warmth and complexity, and peanuts provide welcome crunch.

Preheat the oven to 160°C fan-forced (or 180°C conventional). Grease a large rectangular baking tin (about 33cm x 23cm) and line with baking paper, hanging over the edges (you will use this to lift the slice from the tin).

For the peanut shortbread base, melt the butter in a saucepan over medium-low heat. Remove from the heat, add the peanut butter, sugars and vanilla. Whisk until well combined and the peanut butter has melted. In a large bowl, whisk together the flour, bicarb soda and salt. Make a well in the centre of the dry ingredients, pour in the wet ingredients and mix with a wooden spoon to form a soft dough. Press evenly over the base of the prepared baking tin (you can use the bottom of a glass to do this). Bake for 15 minutes, until golden brown. Set aside to cool a little while you make the caramel.

To make the masala caramel, place all ingredients in a saucepan over medium heat. Cook, stirring occasionally, until melted and smooth. Keep cooking until the caramel thickens slightly and just starts to bubble. Pour the hot caramel over the peanut shortbread base and smooth with the back of a spoon to form an even layer. Return to the oven and bake for a further 20 minutes, until the caramel is golden brown and bubbling (the top of the caramel should be set when you very lightly touch the surface). Leave to cool at room temperature for 30 minutes, then refrigerate for 3 hours, until the caramel is cooled and completely set.

For the chocolate peanut topping, place the chocolate and coconut oil in a heatproof bowl over a saucepan one-third full with simmering water, ensuring the water is not touching the base of the bowl. Gently melt the chocolate into the oil, stirring occasionally until smooth. Pour over the set caramel, spreading evenly with a spatula, and scatter the chopped peanuts over the chocolate. Refrigerate for 1 hour until the chocolate hardens, before cutting into rectangles.

Store in an airtight container at room temperature for up to 4 days.

Note: To roast your own peanuts, place shelled peanuts in a single layer on a baking paper-lined oven tray and roast at 160°C fan-forced (or 180°C conventional) for 15–20 minutes, until golden brown. Rub with a tea towel to remove any skins.

Peanut shortbread base

175g butter, cut into small cubes

120g crunchy peanut butter

100g soft brown sugar

50g caster sugar

1 tsp vanilla extract

300g plain flour

¾ tsp bicarbonate of soda

¼ tsp sea salt

Masala caramel

2 x 395g cans sweetened condensed milk

150g butter, cut into 2cm cubes

120g golden syrup

2 tsp garam masala

¾ tsp sea salt

Chocolate peanut topping

250g milk chocolate, chopped

1 tbsp coconut oil

75g roasted peanuts, roughly chopped (see note)

Lime, apple & poppy seed cake with caramelised coconut topping

Cake batter

165ml canola oil

1 tbsp apple cider vinegar

finely grated zest and freshly squeezed juice (about 100ml) of 4 limes

100g caster sugar

50g soft brown sugar

1 tsp vanilla extract

210g unsweetened natural Greek-style coconut yoghurt

265g plain flour

85g ground almonds

50g desiccated coconut

3 tbsp poppy seeds

2 tsp baking powder

¼ tsp sea salt

2 medium Granny Smith apples, peeled, cored and cut into 1cm chunks (about 180g)

Caramelised coconut topping

100g coconut chips

65g soft brown sugar

50g vegan butter or spread

60ml coconut cream

finely grated zest and freshly squeezed juice of 1 lime

Here the cake is baked then returned to the oven after adding the coconut topping, with the liquid soaking into the cake to make it incredibly moist. This cake is best served on the day of baking, but is still very delicious on all the days after.

Preheat the oven to 160°C fan-forced (or 180°C conventional). Grease a 23cm round springform tin and line with baking paper.

To make the cake, whisk the oil, vinegar, lime zest, juice, caster sugar, brown sugar and vanilla in a large bowl until well combined. Gently stir in the coconut yoghurt. In a separate large bowl, whisk the flour, ground almonds, coconut, poppy seeds, baking powder and salt until evenly combined. Make a well in the centre and pour the wet ingredients into the dry. Mix together until smooth and no specks of flour remain. Finally, fold the chopped apples into the batter until evenly distributed. Spoon into the prepared tin and smooth the top. Bake for 40 minutes, until the cake is only just baked through (a skewer inserted into the centre of the cake should come out just clean).

Make the caramelised coconut topping as the cake is baking. Place all of the ingredients in a saucepan over medium heat. Stir together until the butter has melted and is just starting to bubble.

To finish the cake, remove from the oven and spoon the warm caramelised coconut topping evenly over the surface to completely cover. Drizzle any of the remaining liquid in the pan around the outer edge of the cake. Return to the oven and bake for a further 15–20 minutes, until the top of the coconut topping is a gorgeous deep golden brown. Remove from the oven and place on a wire rack. Leave to cool for 15 minutes before removing the sides of the tin. Leave to cool completely at room temperature.

For serving, transfer to a cake stand or plate. It's best eaten on the day, but any leftovers can be stored in an airtight container at room temperature for up to 3 days.

Chai, date & banana self-saucing pudding with tahini cream

hands-on time	30 mins
total time	1 hour
serves	6

(VE) (S) (S) (A) (W)

Dates bring an almost sticky-date quality to this, their caramel flavour matching with the banana and spices. I often make more Chai spice mix than the recipe requires, to have in the pantry for future desserts when the feeling strikes.

Preheat the oven to 160°C fan-forced (or 180°C conventional). Lightly oil a deep 20–25cm ovenproof baking dish or Dutch oven.

First make the chai spice mix. Whisk the spices together in a bowl to combine. Set aside.

For the pudding batter, place the dates in a bowl and pour over 500ml boiling water. Leave for 10 minutes for the dates to soften. Place the mashed bananas, brown sugar, almond milk, oil and tahini in a large bowl. Beat with an electric mixer (or whisk furiously by hand) for a minute, until well combined. In a separate bowl, sift together the flour, baking powder, bicarb soda, salt and half the chai spice mix. Fold the dry ingredients into the wet mixture until smooth and just combined (there should be no remaining specks of flour). Drain 375ml water from the dates into a saucepan (to use for the sauce) and set aside. Discard any remaining water. Fold the chopped dates into the batter then spoon into the prepared baking dish, smoothing the surface with the back of a spoon.

To make the sauce, bring the date water to the boil over high heat. Remove from the heat and whisk in the sugar, golden syrup and remaining chai spice mix. Carefully pour the hot sauce over the back of a large spoon onto the pudding batter (pouring onto the spoon first avoids splashing or creating holes in the batter).

Bake for 35–40 minutes, until the pudding is golden brown and springs back when lightly touched. There should still be a slight jiggle from the sauce underneath. Remove from the oven and leave to cool for 5 minutes.

To make the tahini cream, open the chilled can of coconut cream, scoop the solidified cream into a bowl and discard any water that has separated. Using an electric hand mixer, beat the cream on high until smooth and whipped. Add the tahini and whisk by hand until smooth.

Serve the pudding warm in bowls, topped with large spoonfuls of tahini cream.

Chai spice mix

2 tsp ground ginger

2 tsp ground cinnamon

1 tsp ground cardamom

1 tsp ground cloves

1 tsp ground allspice

½ tsp ground nutmeg

½ tsp cracked black pepper

Pudding batter

200g dried pitted dates, finely chopped

2 ripe bananas, mashed with a fork

100g soft brown sugar

125ml almond milk

85ml canola oil

1 tbsp tahini

250g plain flour

1 ½ tsp baking powder

1 tsp bicarbonate of soda

¼ tsp sea salt

Chai caramel sauce

100g soft brown sugar

2 tbsp golden or maple syrup

Tahini cream

400g can coconut cream, refrigerated overnight to solidify

2 tbsp tahini

Chilli, chocolate & orange 'impossible' cake

hands-on time	45 mins
total time	1 hour 45 mins (+ cooling time)
serves	12

S S A W

This Mexican-inspired creation sees layers of custard flan and chocolate cake swap places in the tin as they bake. Chilli flakes infuse into the caramel to give a lovely warming heat that complements the orange and chocolate.

Preheat the oven to 160°C fan-forced (or 180°C conventional). Grease a 25cm round Bundt tin generously with butter.

For the chilli caramel, place the caster sugar and 60ml water in a deep saucepan over medium-low heat. Melt the sugar into the water until fully dissolved, then increase the heat to medium-high. Do NOT stir beyond this point. Bring to the boil and cook for 5–10 minutes, to a deep amber colour. Remove from the heat, sprinkle over the chilli flakes, and pour into the base of the prepared tin. Sit the Bundt tin inside a large roasting tin big enough to hold it comfortably.

To infuse the milk for the orange flan, place the evaporated milk, orange zest and vanilla in a small saucepan over medium-low heat. Heat until just starting to steam (you do not want the milk to bubble), then remove from the heat and set aside for 15 minutes to deeply infuse the milk.

To make the cake batter, beat the butter and both sugars in a large bowl using an electric hand or stand mixer (with the paddle attachment) for 3 minutes, until light and fluffy. Add the eggs and vanilla and mix until just combined. In a separate bowl, whisk together the flour, cocoa, baking powder, bicarb soda, orange zest, ground chilli and salt. In a small bowl, whisk together the buttermilk and orange juice. Mix half the flour mixture into the butter mixture, followed by half the orange buttermilk. Repeat, adding the remaining flour mixture then orange buttermilk, mixing until just incorporated and smooth. Spoon the cake batter over the chilli caramel in the Bundt tin, smoothing the top with the back of a spoon.

For the orange flan, remove the orange zest from the evaporated milk. Pour the infused evaporated milk, condensed milk, cream cheese and eggs into a food processor or blender and blitz for about 20 seconds, until smooth. Gently pour the flan mixture over the back of a spoon onto the cake batter.

To bake, lightly grease a piece of foil with butter and tent loosely over the Bundt tin, wrapping tightly around the edges to seal. Pour boiling water into the roasting tin to come just under halfway up the sides of the Bundt tin. Carefully place in the oven and bake for 1 hour, or until a skewer inserted into the cake comes out clean.

Chilli caramel

200g caster sugar

1 tsp chilli flakes

Orange flan

340ml can evaporated milk

peeled zest of 1 orange

1 tsp vanilla extract

395g can condensed milk

150g cream cheese, at room temperature, chopped

4 eggs

Cake batter

125g butter, softened to room temperature, chopped

100g caster sugar

100g soft brown sugar

2 eggs

1 tsp vanilla extract

200g plain flour

75g cocoa powder, sifted

1 tsp baking powder

1 tsp bicarbonate of soda

finely grated zest of 1 orange

½ tsp ground chilli

½ tsp sea salt

185ml buttermilk

60ml freshly squeezed orange juice

Remove from the oven, lift the Bundt tin out of the roasting tin and place onto a wire rack. Remove the foil and leave to cool at room temperature for 1 hour, until completely cool. Carefully invert the cake onto a large, round platter with a lip (some of the caramel will likely pool on the platter around the cake). If any of the caramel has stuck to the bottom of the Bundt tin, return the tin to the oven for 10 minutes until it melts, then drizzle around the top of the cake. This will then harden and give you an incredible crunchy topping.

Serve at room temperature or refrigerate and serve chilled (my preference) – both are delicious.

Matcha & pistachio amaretti

hands-on time	15 mins
total time	1 hour 10 mins
makes	15 small cookies

(GF)   S S A W

In the style of Italian amaretti, these biscuits are wonderfully chewy due to a base of egg whites and ground nuts. Matcha and pistachio are buddies in green and a dangerously moreish combination, so if ingredients are on hand, this recipe is always worth doubling.

Place the pistachios in a food processor and blitz until finely ground. Transfer to a large bowl, add the ground almonds, caster sugar, matcha and salt, whisking to combine. In a separate bowl, use an electric hand mixer to beat the egg whites until soft peaks form. Add the egg whites and vanilla to the dry ingredients. Use a spatula to gently fold together to make a soft, slightly sticky paste. Cover the bowl and refrigerate for 40 minutes, so that the mixture can be rolled into balls without sticking to your hands.

Preheat the oven to 150°C fan-forced (or 170°C conventional). Line 2 oven trays with baking paper.

Sift the icing sugar into a shallow bowl. Roll the chilled dough into small balls (about 30g each). Roll the balls in the icing sugar to coat generously. Place on the oven trays spaced at least 4cm apart, as they may spread a little as they bake.

Bake for 15–20 minutes, until cracked, fragrant and just starting to turn lightly golden brown at the edges.

Leave to cool on the trays for 10 minutes, before carefully moving to a wire rack to cool completely. Store in an airtight container for up to 3 days.

100g pistachio kernels
110g ground almonds
200g caster sugar
1 tbsp matcha powder
pinch of sea salt
65g egg whites (about 2)
1 tsp vanilla bean paste
75g icing sugar

Christmas meringue roulade with rosé cherries & chantilly cream

hands-on time	1 hour
total time	1 hour 15 mins
serves	10

(GF) (S)

An exciting take on a classic. The meringue is baked thin and rectangular then rolled up to form a roulade. It's flavoured with a Christmas spice mix and filled with cream and rosé-poached cherries. Hark thou hear the angels sing.

Preheat the oven to 190°C fan-forced (or 210°C conventional). Grease a Swiss roll tin or large rectangular baking tin (about 33cm x 23cm) and line with baking paper.

For the meringue roulade, place the egg whites in a clean large bowl. Using an electric hand or stand mixer, beat the egg whites on high speed until they form soft peaks. While beating continuously, gradually add the caster sugar, 1 tbsp at a time, followed by the brown sugar. Once all the sugar has been added, continue beating for a further 5 minutes to form a beautifully stiff, thick and glossy meringue. In a separate bowl, whisk together the ground spices, then add to the meringue and beat on medium speed until evenly mixed through. In a small cup, whisk together the vinegar and cornflour and add to the meringue, again beating on medium speed until well combined. Spoon the meringue into the prepared tin and gently spread out with the back of a spoon to form an even layer, being careful not to deflate the meringue. Place into the oven and immediately lower the temperature to 170°C fan-forced (or 190°C conventional). Bake for 10 minutes, then reduce the temperature again to 140°C fan-forced (or 160°C conventional) and bake for a further 15 minutes. The meringue will have puffed up and have a crusty surface. Remove from the oven and leave to cool for 5 minutes to allow the meringue to deflate a little. Place a piece of baking paper just larger than the size of the meringue on your work surface, long side facing towards you. Working quickly and carefully, invert the meringue onto the baking paper and carefully peel the baking paper from the meringue. Leave to cool completely at room temperature.

Meringue roulade

170g egg whites (about 5)
200g caster sugar
65g soft brown sugar
1 tsp ground cinnamon
½ tsp ground cardamom
½ tsp ground ginger
½ tsp ground star anise
½ tsp ground allspice
1 tsp white wine vinegar
1 tsp cornflour

Rosé cherries

300g fresh or frozen pitted
cherries, halved

100g caster sugar

125ml rosé wine

freshly squeezed juice of
½ lemon

Chantilly cream

250ml cream

2 tbsp icing sugar, sifted

1 ½ tsp vanilla extract

For the rosé cherries, place the cherries and sugar in a heavy-based saucepan over medium heat. Stir through and warm for a few minutes, until the sugar is dissolved. Pour in the rosé and lemon juice and increase the heat to medium-high. Bring to the boil and cook vigorously for about 15 minutes, stirring occasionally and squashing the cherries a little, until the cherries are softened and the liquid has reduced to a syrupy, almost runny jam-like consistency (remembering the syrup will thicken as it cools). Transfer to a bowl and set aside to cool.

For the chantilly cream, using an electric hand mixer, beat together the cream, icing sugar and vanilla until thickened and soft peaks form (be careful not to overmix).

To roll the roulade, spread three-quarters of the Chantilly cream over the surface of the cooled meringue, leaving a 2cm border on the long edge furthest away from you without cream (as the cream will spill onto this as you roll the meringue). Dot three-quarters of the rosé cherries over the top of the cream. With the long edge facing you, roll up the meringue tightly, using the baking paper to help you and gently removing this as you go, to form a log. Carefully transfer the roulade, seam side down, to a serving platter or board. Spoon the remaining cream down the length of the roulade, spreading along the top with the back of a spoon, and top with the remaining cherries. Slice and serve. This is best eaten on the day, but any leftovers will keep in the fridge for up to 2 days.

Sustain

Basics & staples

The recipes ahead have been referenced throughout the book, as a key component to a greater recipe, or as a highly recommended accompaniment. They have all become staples in my kitchen, as much for their versatility as their individual merit, and my hope is that they will find a similar place in your own repertoire.

Many are doughs and crusts that form a structural foundation, such as Ginger sweet shortcrust pastry (page 222) or Sunset wraps (page 230). Others are pickles and preserves that feature widely, whether within the method, like Preserved lemons (page 218), or as a serving suggestion at the close, such as Pickled chillies (page 218).

Recipes that form the backbone of this book; recipes that *sustain*.

Basic fresh pasta

hands-on time	15 mins
total time	45 mins
makes	435g, serves 4

You'll be blown away by how simple it is to make fresh pasta. This recipe can be doubled to feed a crowd, or flavoured and coloured with puréed blanched spinach or roasted beetroot purée. I inherited my granddad's old Italian pasta machine, and it's become one of my favourite activities to invite some friends over and make pasta together.

200g '00' flour

75g fine semolina

160g eggs (about 3)

Whisk the flour and semolina in a bowl to combine. Tip out onto a clean work surface into a large raised mound and create a hollow in the centre. Crack the eggs into the hollow, then whisk the eggs with a fork until evenly combined. Using your fingers, carefully mix the eggs into the flour to form a firm but kneadable dough – be careful as the dam may break and egg spill out from the flour. Knead the dough by hand for 8 minutes, until smooth and it springs back when prodded. Wrap loosely with clingfilm and set aside to rest at room temperature for 30 minutes.

Divide the dough into 4 pieces. Take 1 piece, roll out into a rectangle thin enough to go through the widest setting on your pasta machine, and roll through the machine twice, dusting with a little flour as you go. Repeat, gradually reducing the width setting on the machine, until the desired thickness is reached (usually the second narrowest setting). Cut the sheet of pasta in half if it is becoming too long to manage. Cut the pasta to the desired shape, using the appropriate attachment on the pasta machine, or a sharp knife. Cook the pasta in a large saucepan of salted boiling water for a couple of minutes (depending on its size), stirring occasionally to separate the strands, until al dente.

Alternatively, if you don't have a pasta machine, on a lightly floured surface using a rolling pin, roll out the pasta as thinly as possible. You will need to lift the dough and re-flour the surface regularly, to prevent the dough from sticking. Cut and cook as above.

Coconut rice

300g basmati rice

250ml coconut cream

This is my speedy, no-fuss recipe for coconut rice that follows the simple absorption method my parents first taught me as a child. To ensure the rice grains are separate when cooked, remove the excess starch by rinsing the rice before cooking. You can flavour your rice – a combination of cumin seeds, saffron, caramelised onions and sultanas is a favourite.

Place the rice in a sieve and rinse under cold running water, until the water draining from the rice runs clear. Transfer the rice to a saucepan and pour over the coconut cream and 300ml cold water. Cover the saucepan with a lid and bring to the boil over high heat. Do NOT remove the lid during the cooking process. As soon as the rice is bubbling vigorously, reduce the temperature to low and leave to simmer for 14 minutes. Remove from the heat and leave the rice to stand (with the lid still on) for a further 10 minutes. Remove the lid and fluff up the rice with a fork.

For lemon & coriander rice

Finely grate the zest of 1 lemon and set aside. Slice the lemon into thin discs and add to the saucepan with the rice, coconut cream and water before cooking. Once the rice is cooked, remove the lemon slices, fluff up with a fork, then stir through the grated lemon zest and 1 large handful of coriander leaves before serving.

How to sterilise a jar

Make the most of produce when it is in season. A great way to use up late-season fruit and veg, or a glut from the garden, is by making chutneys, jams, pickles and preserves.

You can sterilise glass jars and their lids by any one of these methods:

A. wash well, then place upright in an oven preheated to 120°C and heat for 20 minutes (my preferred method). Fill while hot.

B. place in a large saucepan of boiling water for 10 minutes, then drain upside down on a clean tea towel. Fill while hot.

C. place through a hot dishwasher cycle, then drain upside down on a clean tea towel. Fill while hot.

Once sterilised, pour the hot pickle or preserve into the jars and seal with their lids immediately. Leave to cool at room temperature and store in your pantry in a cool, dark place. Refrigerate once opened.

hands-on time	10 mins
total time	10 mins
makes	150g

(VE) (GF)

Firehouse rose harissa

1 tsp cumin seeds

1 tsp coriander seeds

1 tsp fennel seeds

3 tbsp olive oil

10 long red chillies, deseeded and finely chopped

4 cloves garlic, finely chopped

1 red capsicum, cored, deseeded and diced

1 tbsp apple cider vinegar

2 tsp rose water

½ tsp sea salt

½ tsp ground chipotle chilli

freshly squeezed juice of ½ lemon

This is my version of the traditional North African chilli paste. Use chillies based on your heat preference, and when cooking with it, start with a little – a tablespoonful goes a long way.

Toast the seeds in a frying pan over medium-high heat for 1–2 minutes, until fragrant and starting to pop. Use a mortar and pestle and grind to a reasonably fine powder. Heat 1 tbsp of the oil in the frying pan over medium heat. Add the chillies, garlic and capsicum and fry for 5 minutes, until the garlic is starting to become golden and the capsicum has softened. Transfer to a bowl and add the spices, remaining olive oil and the remaining ingredients. Using a stick blender (or similar) blitz until a relatively smooth paste is reached.

Transfer to a sterilised airtight jar and refrigerate for up to 2 weeks. Use 1 tbsp of this versatile chilli paste to add a serious kick of flavour and heat.

Pickled chillies

hands-on time	10 mins
total time	10 mins
makes	1 medium–large jar

These pickles are an excellent addition to recipes such as my Beetroot & jackfruit chilli with sour yoghurt (page 150) or Chilli basil beef with black bean rice (page 102).

Toast the seeds and peppercorns in a frying pan over medium heat for 2 minutes, until fragrant. Use a mortar and pestle to roughly grind. Transfer the ground mixture to a medium–large sterilised jar, along with the sliced chillies and kaffir lime leaves. Place the vinegar, sugar and salt in a saucepan with 185ml water. Bring to the boil over medium-high heat, then reduce the heat to medium and simmer for 3 minutes. Pour the hot liquid into the jar to cover the chillies completely. Screw on the lid and leave to cool completely at room temperature. Store in a cool dark place for up to 6 months, then refrigerate once opened.

1 tbsp fennel seeds

1 tbsp coriander seeds

2 tsp black mustard seeds

1 tsp black peppercorns

150g green chillies, sliced

2 kaffir lime leaves

185ml apple cider vinegar

1 tbsp caster sugar

1 tbsp sea salt

Preserved lemons

hands-on time	10 mins
total time	10 mins
makes	1 medium–large jar

Preserved lemons are commonly used in North African and Indian cooking. I prefer to use the skin, rather than the flesh, as in Preserved lemon teriyaki salmon with spring greens & soba (page 119) and Breakfast gözleme with preserved lemon mayo (page 38).

Sterilise a medium–large glass jar (about 800ml) and its lid. Cut an 'X' cross into each lemon, stopping when you are three-quarters of the way through so that the lemons remain intact at the base but are separated into quarters. Pack 1 tbsp salt into each lemon, then tightly pack the salted lemons into the sterilised jar, pressing down with the end of a wooden spoon to extract as much juice out of the lemons as possible. Add the coriander seeds, cardamom pods, peppercorns and bay leaf. Using the wooden spoon, muddle the seeds with the lemons. Squeeze in enough extra lemon juice to cover the lemons completely, seal the jar and place in a cool, dark, dry place for 3–4 weeks. Move to the refrigerator and use as desired. They will keep in the fridge for 3 months.

6 lemons, plus extra for additional juice

6 tbsp coarse sea salt

1 tsp coriander seeds

10 green cardamom pods, crushed open

10 whole peppercorns

1 bay leaf

hands-on time	5 mins
total time	25 mins
makes	150g

Quick-pickled cucumber

1 tbsp coriander seeds

½ large telegraph cucumber, thinly sliced (with a mandoline if you have one)

125ml apple cider vinegar

60ml freshly squeezed orange juice

1 tbsp maple syrup

¼ tsp sea salt

The quick-pickling method is perfect when you want pickled cucumber on demand, or you can make it a few days in advance and store it in the refrigerator until needed.

Use a mortar and pestle to lightly crush the coriander seeds. Place the coriander seeds and the remaining ingredients into a jar and stir to combine. Cover and set aside for at least 20 minutes to allow the cucumber to pickle. Refrigerate until ready to eat. This will keep in the fridge for up to 1 week.

hands-on time	10 mins
total time	20 mins
makes	400g

Coriander onions

1 tbsp coriander seeds

1 tsp black peppercorns

3 red onions, thinly sliced

185ml apple cider vinegar

50g soft brown sugar

½ lemon, cut in half

1 tsp sea salt

Pickled onions can bring an instant flavour lift to an otherwise ordinary dish. Coriander seeds have a wonderful citrus taste and aroma that shines through in these onions.

Toast the coriander seeds and peppercorns in a saucepan over medium heat, for 1–2 minutes until fragrant. Stir in the remaining ingredients, increase the heat to high and bring to the boil. Once bubbling rapidly, reduce the heat to medium, place a lid on the saucepan and simmer vigorously for 15 minutes. Remove from the heat and set aside to cool to room temperature.

If serving immediately, remove the lemon and drain the excess liquid. Serve with your favourite meal – like my Ultimate vegan burgers (page 164). If making in advance, spoon the onions and any excess liquid into a storage container or jar and refrigerate for up to 2 weeks.

Tomato, date & tamarind chutney

hands-on time	1 hour 15 mins
total time	1 hour 15 mins
makes	4 medium-sized jars

This chutney has umami from tomatoes, sweetness from dates, and sourness from tamarind. It's perfect with crackers and cheese (particularly blue vein), or on the side of an omelette or frittata, like my Massaman potato frittata (page 124).

Toast the cumin seeds and peppercorns in a frying pan over medium heat for 1–2 minutes, until fragrant. Use a mortar and pestle to grind to as fine a powder as you can be bothered making. Heat the olive oil in a large, heavy-based saucepan over medium heat. Add the onions and sauté for 5 minutes, until starting to soften. Add the ground cumin and peppercorns, paprika, mustard seeds, garlic, chillies and ginger. Stir through the onions and fry for a further 2 minutes, until the garlic is starting to lightly brown. Chop the tomatoes as finely as possible – if you have a food processor, it is easiest to blitz them in this. Add the tomatoes and remaining ingredients to the saucepan and stir through, ensuring you scrape up any onions and spices sticking to the bottom of the pan. Increase the heat to medium-high and bring to the boil. Reduce the heat to medium and simmer vigorously for 1 hour, until nicely thickened, stirring occasionally to ensure the chutney doesn't catch on the bottom of the saucepan.

Pour the hot chutney into four sterilised jars and seal. Store unopened at room temperature for 3-6 months for the flavour to develop. Refrigerate once opened.

2 tsp cumin seeds

1 tsp whole black peppercorns

2 tbsp olive oil

2 red onions, finely chopped

2 tsp paprika

2 tsp black mustard seeds

4 cloves garlic, finely chopped

2 red chillies, finely chopped

2 tbsp finely grated fresh ginger

1.5kg tomatoes, stems removed

250ml apple cider vinegar

125ml white wine vinegar

200g dried pitted dates, finely chopped

200g soft brown sugar

150g caster sugar

3 tbsp tamarind paste

2 tsp sea salt

Raspberry & lemon jam

hands-on time	15 mins
total time	15 mins
makes	3 medium-sized jars

(VE) (GF)

750g frozen raspberries

finely grated zest and freshly squeezed juice of 2 lemons

700g caster sugar

It's a whānau tradition every Christmas to make a dessert called Turkey Pudding. It begins with making a sponge roll, which is slathered with raspberry & lemon jam and rolled up. This one's for you, Grandma Peg.

Place a small plate in the freezer to chill (you will use this later to test if your jam is set). Place the raspberries, lemon zest and juice in a medium–large saucepan over medium heat. Warm for a few minutes, breaking down the raspberries with a wooden spoon, until the raspberries start to soften and become mushy. Add the sugar, stir through and warm for 2 minutes until dissolved, then increase the heat to high. Bring to the boil and once bubbling vigorously, cook for 8–10 minutes, stirring occasionally, until the jam has thickened nicely (I suggest wearing an apron as the jam can splutter a little). To test that the jam is ready, place a tsp of the hot jam onto the chilled plate. Cool for about 2 minutes, then push your finger into the jam. If it is set it should wrinkle and feel thickened.

When the jam is ready, pour the hot jam into sterilised jars and seal tightly. Store at room temperature for up to 6 months. Refrigerate once opened.

Rose & orange roasted rhubarb

hands-on time	5 mins
total time	20 mins
serves	6

I like to roast my rhubarb, as it softens gently while retaining its form, with hints of rose and orange in the roasting syrup for a little floral and a little sweet.

Preheat the oven to 160°C fan-forced (or 180°C conventional).

Place the rhubarb in a baking dish or roasting tin big enough to sit in a single layer. Add the remaining ingredients and toss with the rhubarb to coat. Bake for 15–20 minutes, until the rhubarb is just starting to soften but retaining its structure. Set aside to cool in the syrup. Transfer to an airtight container and refrigerate for up to 5 days.

Serve with your favourite dessert, granola, yoghurt or bircher muesli, as seen in my A-little-luxe overnight bircher (page 20).

400g rhubarb, cut into 5cm pieces
50g caster sugar
finely grated zest of 1 orange
60ml freshly squeezed orange juice
1 tbsp rose water

Ginger sweet shortcrust pastry

hands-on time	10 mins
total time	10 mins (+ 1 hour chill time)
makes	enough for one 23–25cm tart

Making shortcrust pastry is simple. This pastry is perfect for tarts and pie crusts, like my Grapefruit & thyme meringue pie (page 196). Instead of ground ginger, you can add your own spices or herbs, or leave it plain.

Whisk the flour, icing sugar and ginger in a bowl until evenly combined. Add the butter, and using your hands, rub the butter into the dry ingredients until it resembles a coarse breadcrumb texture – the odd coarser chunk of butter is okay.

Make a well in the centre, add the egg yolk and about 2 tbsp very cold water, 1 tbsp at a time, to just form a soft dough. Gather the dough together and press into a thick disc. Wrap loosely in clingfilm and refrigerate for a minimum of 1 hour before using.

If you're not using the pastry immediately, you can wrap it in clingfilm and keep in the refrigerator for 3 days or in the freezer for up to 1 month.

225g plain flour
50g icing sugar
1 tsp ground ginger
150g chilled butter, cut into small cubes
1 egg yolk

hands-on time	1 hour
total time	1 hour
makes	200g

(GF)

Caramelised white chocolate

200g white chocolate (minimum 29% cocoa butter), cut into small chunks

When you roast white chocolate, the sugars caramelise and create an intense butterscotch quality. Caramelised white chocolate is readily available in supermarkets, but making your own beats the store-bought stuff.

Preheat the oven to 110°C fan-forced (or 130°C conventional).

Place the chopped white chocolate on a rimmed oven tray in a single layer. Roast for 10 minutes, then remove from the oven. Use a spatula to give the chocolate a good stir, then smooth out evenly. Return to the oven and repeat this process of roasting, stirring and smoothing every 10 minutes, until the chocolate is deep golden brown in colour. It will take about 1 hour in total. The chocolate will appear grainy and lumpy during the process, but following this method it will eventually melt together. Remove from the oven, transfer to an airtight container and leave to cool until solid. Store at room temperature for future use.

Two-hour pizza dough

hands-on time	20 mins
total time	2 hours
makes	3 large pizzas

For a quick yeast-based pizza dough, you can't get much better than this. When it comes to toppings, I often find that less is more, and I've listed some of my favourite combinations below. Enjoy.

12g active dried yeast

15g caster sugar

525g high grade flour

10g sea salt

1 tbsp olive oil

Whisk 375ml warm water with the yeast and caster sugar in a bowl. Leave in a warm place for 10–15 minutes, until frothy. Sift the flour and salt into a large bowl. Add the yeast mixture to the flour and mix to a soft, slightly sticky dough. Tip out onto a clean work surface, and using your hands, knead for 10 minutes, pushing the dough into the work surface with the heel of your hand and stretching and tearing it as you go. Avoid using any additional flour while kneading – the dough will stick to your hands a little at the start but as the gluten develops you will be left with a smooth, satiny dough.

Pour the oil into the bowl, place the dough in the centre and turn to coat the surface of the dough with the oil. Cover the bowl with a tea towel and leave in a warm place to prove for about 1 ½ hours or until doubled in size. Punch down the dough to deflate, divide into 3 pieces (for 3 large pizzas), and roll into balls. The pizza dough is ready to use immediately, store in the refrigerator for up to 5 days, or the freezer for up to 3 months.

To assemble and bake your pizzas, preheat the oven to 230°C fan-forced (or 250°C conventional). Place pizza stones or oven trays in the oven as it heats – this will ensure your pizzas have a crispy base.

On a lightly floured surface, using your hands, roll and stretch each piece of dough to your desired size. Transfer each pizza base to a lightly floured sheet of baking paper, big enough to cover the pizza stone or oven tray. Top the pizza bases with your desired toppings. Remove the hot pizza stones from the oven and holding the ends of the baking paper, transfer the pizzas/baking paper onto the hot stones. Bake for 10–15 minutes, until the base is crispy and the toppings golden.

Pizza topping suggestions

- Olive oil base, thinly sliced lemon, sumac, sliced olives, mozzarella, parmesan, thyme

- Pizza sauce (page 225) base, sliced pepperoni, capers, chilli flakes, mozzarella, basil

- Olive oil base, thinly sliced pears, blue cheese, mozzarella, walnuts, rocket

hands-on time	10 mins
total time	25 mins
makes	1 medium–large jar

Pizza sauce

4 tbsp olive oil

½ small red onion, finely chopped

4 cloves garlic, finely chopped

400g can chopped tomatoes

120g tomato paste

1 large handful basil leaves, finely chopped

1 tsp cracked black pepper

1 tsp sea salt, or to taste

This sauce can be slathered over the base of a pizza or used as a quick tomato pasta sauce. Instead of basil you can use other fresh herbs, such as oregano or flat-leaf parsley.

Heat the olive oil in a saucepan over medium heat. Add the onion and sauté for 5 minutes, until starting to soften. Add the garlic and cook for a further 2 minutes until the garlic turns light golden. Add the remaining ingredients, increase the heat to medium-high, and bring to the boil. Once bubbling like a cauldron, reduce the heat to medium-low and simmer for 15 minutes until reduced and thickened. Remove from the heat, adjust seasoning to taste, and blitz with a stick blender, or similar, to form a smooth sauce. Leave to cool and use immediately, or spoon into a jar and refrigerate for up to 2 weeks.

Bestest bao

hands-on time	1 hour
total time	2 hours 30 mins
makes	12

(VE)

10g active dried yeast

2 tbsp caster sugar

2 tbsp canola oil, plus extra for brushing

450g plain flour

2 tsp baking powder

½ tsp sea salt

Bao are the most popular hand-held party food in my kitchen. Because of their softness, it's worth including texture and structure in the filling – such as the crispy tofu in my Five spice tofu bao with sesame-orange sauce, pickles & sticky cashews (page 79).

To make the dough, whisk 125ml warm water with the yeast and 1 tbsp of the caster sugar in a bowl. Leave in a warm place for 10–15 minutes until frothy. In a cup, whisk the canola oil with another 125ml warm water. In a large bowl, whisk the flour, baking powder, salt and remaining 1 tbsp caster sugar. Make a well in the centre. Add the yeast mixture and oil mixture to the dry ingredients, and using your hands, mix to a soft, slightly sticky dough. Tip out onto a clean work surface and knead for 10 minutes, until soft, smooth and bouncy (avoid adding any extra flour as you knead). Form the dough into a ball and place in a lightly oiled bowl. Cover the bowl with a damp tea towel and leave in a warm place for about 1 ½ hours, or until doubled in size.

Cut 12 10cm squares of baking paper. Punch down the dough to deflate, and tip it out onto a clean work surface. Knead for a few seconds to knock out the air. Divide into 12 equal pieces (about 60g each) and shape into balls. Take each ball and gently roll out into an oval disc, measuring 9cm x 12cm, and lightly brush the surface with a little canola oil. Fold each oval in half to form a halfmoon shape and place onto the baking paper squares on a tray. Loosely cover with clingfilm and leave to prove for 30 minutes at room temperature, so that they puff up a little.

To cook the bao, set a steamer (preferably made of bamboo and 2 tiers) over a saucepan of simmering water. Pick up each bao, using the corners of the baking paper, and place them (on their paper) in a single layer in each tier of the steamer, making sure they do not touch each other or the sides of the steamer. Cover and steam for 10 minutes, until puffy, soft and cooked through. Remove the steamer from the heat, let the buns cool slightly, then remove from the steamer and repeat until all bao have been cooked. Serve warm.

Note: You can make the bao in advance and freeze them until needed. Steam the buns as directed, allow to cool to room temperature then place on a baking paper-lined tray. Freeze for 1–2 hours until solid then transfer to a resealable bag or container and freeze for up to 3 months. To reheat, steam the frozen buns for 5–10 minutes, until warmed through completely.

hands–on time	45 mins
total time	3 hours 30 mins
makes	8 large buns

Vegan burger buns

Tangzhong starter

25g high grade flour

85ml cold water

Dough

250ml warm almond milk

12g active dried yeast

1 tbsp caster sugar

75g coconut oil

50g tahini

450g high grade flour

1 tbsp curry powder

finely grated zest of ½ lemon

10g sea salt

'Egg' wash

2 tbsp almond milk

1 tbsp maple syrup

2 tbsp white sesame seeds

2 tbsp black sesame seeds

A decent burger needs a decent bun. Tangzhong roux keeps the buns soft and fluffy, while coconut oil and tahini give a brioche-like quality. I add a little curry powder and lemon zest to give the dough a flavour lift.

First make the tangzhong starter. Place the flour and water in a small saucepan and whisk until smooth. Cook over medium heat for a few minutes, stirring regularly, until thickened to a paste. Transfer to a small bowl and leave to cool to room temperature.

For the dough, whisk the warm milk, yeast and caster sugar in a small bowl. Leave for 10–15 minutes in a warm place until the yeast is frothy. Heat the coconut oil and tahini in a small saucepan over low heat, stirring until melted and combined. Set aside to cool slightly.

Whisk the flour, curry powder, lemon zest and salt in a large bowl and make a well in the centre. Add the yeast mixture, tahini mixture and tangzhong starter and gently mix to form a soft, slightly sticky dough. Tip out onto a clean work surface and knead for 10 minutes, until the dough is soft, satiny and elastic. The dough will stick to your hands initially but avoid using any extra flour in the kneading process. Alternatively, you can mix and knead the dough in a stand mixer with the dough hook attachment at medium speed. Form the dough into a large ball and return to the mixing bowl. Cover with a damp tea towel and leave in a warm place for about 1 ½ hours, or until doubled in size.

Push down the dough to deflate and divide into 8 pieces (about 100g each). On a clean work surface, roll each piece of dough into a ball, by lightly pushing and turning the dough with the palm of one hand, cupping it slightly to form a ball. Place onto 2 baking paper-lined oven trays, evenly spaced at least 5cm apart. Cover loosely with clingfilm (you want to leave space for the buns to rise) and leave in a warm place for 1 hour, until risen and almost doubled in size.

Meanwhile, preheat the oven to 160°C fan-forced (or 180°C conventional).

For the 'egg' wash, whisk the almond milk and maple syrup in a cup. In a separate cup, mix together the black and white sesame seeds.

Gently brush the buns evenly with the 'egg' wash and sprinkle generously with sesame seeds. Bake for 25–30 minutes, swapping the trays halfway through so they cook evenly, until golden brown and baked through (the bottom of a bun will sound hollow when tapped). Leave to cool to room temperature. Use straight away or store in an airtight container for up to 3 days. Warm before eating.

Corn tortillas

hands-on time	30 mins
total time	1 hour
makes	16 small tortillas

These tortillas are made with masa harina, a cornmeal that can be found at wholefoods or specialty food stores. There is no need to buy a tortilla press – my method achieves a similar result.

275g masa harina

½ tsp sea salt

First make the tortilla dough. Place the masa harina and salt in a bowl. Pour in 375ml hot water and mix to form a soft, slightly tacky dough. Cover with a tea towel and set aside to rest for 30 minutes.

To cook the tortillas, cut out 4 15cm squares of baking paper. Place a large frying pan over high heat. Take 35–40g of tortilla dough and roll into a ball. Place between 2 squares of the baking paper, and use the base of a heavy frying pan or a rolling pin to flatten or roll out to a thin tortilla, 12–15cm in diameter. Carefully remove the top piece of baking paper and then flip the tortilla into the hot dry frying pan (with the remaining baking paper facing upwards). After 30 seconds, carefully remove the baking paper then cook for a further 30 seconds. Carefully flip the tortilla and cook for 60 seconds on the other side. Transfer to a plate and cover with a tea towel. Repeat with the remaining tortilla dough to make about 16 tortillas – as one is cooking, roll out the next. Stack on top of each other as they are cooked and keep covered with the tea towel to keep them warm and soft.

Serve stuffed with your favourite fillings – these are perfect for my Portobello tacos with roasted cherry salsa & avocado cream (page 46).

Note: These tortillas are best eaten fresh, but if made in advance, leave the tortillas to cool completely, then transfer to an airtight ziplock bag (with the air pressed out) and refrigerate for up to 3 days. Warm the tortillas in a hot dry frying pan, for 30 seconds on each side, before eating.

hands-on time	15 mins
total time	1 hour 30 mins
makes	enough for 1 23–25cm pie

Rough puff pastry

300g high grade flour

¾ tsp sea salt

250g frozen butter

Frozen butter reduces the time it takes to rub butter into flour, and the streaks of cold butter allow the pastry to keep its layers. Puff pastry is excellent for savoury pies such as the Black pepper & paneer pie with mango salsa (page 142).

Sift the flour and salt into a large bowl. Grate the frozen butter into the flour. Using your hands, very loosely rub the grated butter into the flour so that it is evenly coated. Make a well in the centre and add 80ml cold water. Mix together gently with your hands, and gradually add up to another 35ml cold water if needed to form a rough, firm but kneadable dough with streaks of butter through it. Cover loosely with clingfilm and refrigerate for 20 minutes.

On a lightly floured surface, roll out the dough into a 40 x 20cm rectangle. With the short edge facing you, fold the top edge of the dough towards the centre then fold the bottom edge over the top to form a three-layered envelope. Give the dough a quarter turn. Roll out the dough again to a 40 x 20cm rectangle. Fold again into an envelope as before. Cover with clingfilm and refrigerate for 20 minutes. Return the dough to the floured surface, roll out and fold into an envelope twice more as before, rotating the dough a quarter turn after each fold. Cover with clingfilm and return the folded dough to the refrigerator to rest for a minimum of 30 minutes or until needed.

Note: The pastry can be made ahead of time, wrapped in clingfilm, and kept in the refrigerator for 3 days or the freezer for up to 1 month.

Sunset wraps

hands-on time	15 mins
total time	35 mins
makes	8 medium–large wraps

Wraps are a super staple to have on hand for when you need to whip up something fast. These tortillas have a yellow hue from the spices I like to flavour them with, but you can change the spices to make these your own.

To make the dough, whisk the flour, turmeric, paprika, cumin and salt in a large bowl. Make a well in the centre and add the oil and 250ml cold water. Using your hands, mix together until shaggy then tip out onto a lightly floured surface and knead for a couple of minutes to form a soft, smooth dough. Cover and set aside for 20 minutes to rest.

To cook the wraps, place a large frying pan over high heat. Divide the dough evenly into 8 pieces and roll into balls. On a floured surface, use a rolling pin to roll one ball of dough into a large, thin round, 20–25cm in diameter. Carefully lift into the hot pan and cook for 40 seconds on one side (at this stage there should be bubbles that start to form under the surface). Flip the tortilla and cook for a further 20 seconds on the other side. Transfer the tortilla to a board or plate and cover with a tea towel (the wrap should still be relatively soft so it can be folded without falling apart). Repeat with the remaining dough to make 8 wraps, rolling out the next wrap as the previous one is cooking. Stack on top of each other as they are cooked and keep covered with the tea towel to keep them warm and soft.

Serve stuffed with your favourite fillings, or use for enchiladas (page 168). If making in advance, leave to cool completely, then transfer to a large airtight ziplock bag (with the air pressed out) and refrigerate for up to 1 week.

450g plain flour
2 tsp ground turmeric
2 tsp ground paprika
1 tsp ground cumin
10g sea salt
60ml olive oil

Yoghurt flatbreads

hands-on time	25 mins
total time	40 mins
makes	4 large flatbreads

1 tbsp coriander seeds

225g plain flour

2 tsp baking powder

½ tsp sea salt

1 tsp dried mint

1 tsp dried sage

210g unsweetened natural Greek-style coconut yoghurt

These vegan flatbreads are perfect for dipping in Harissa baked beans (page 103), scooping up Cilbir eggs (page 28) or being stuffed and rolled, like in my Spiced lamb flatbreads (page 107).

To make the dough, toast the coriander seeds in a frying pan over medium-high heat for a couple of minutes, until fragrant. Use a mortar and pestle to grind the seeds a little until crushed. Transfer the crushed seeds to a large bowl, add the flour, baking powder, salt and herbs and whisk together with a fork. Pour in the yoghurt and mix to form a soft dough. Knead on a clean work surface for 2 minutes, then return to the bowl, cover with a tea towel and leave to rest for 15 minutes.

Divide the dough into 4 equal parts and roll into balls. On a lightly floured surface, use a rolling pin to roll out a ball of dough to a 20cm round. Heat a large frying pan over medium-high heat. Transfer the flatbread to the hot pan and cook for 2 minutes. When large bubbles start to rise underneath the dough, turn and cook for a further 2 minutes. Transfer to a plate and cover with a tea towel to keep warm. Repeat with the remaining dough to make 4 large flatbreads.

What's on the menu?

While I often like to get wild and serve distinctly different dishes together, sometimes you want a menu that lends itself to a theme or occasion. Below are a few menu suggestions to get your own ideas flowing – there are no rules here, merely inspiration. When cooking for guests, always flick through the recipes beforehand to make sure you have all the necessary ingredients, and to see what you can make in advance – reduce the stress and give yourself time to enjoy the company.

Date-night dinner for two

Pumpkin, persimmon & ginger soup with Cajun seeds (page 116)

Coffee & cardamom braised beef cheeks (page 163) + Basic fresh pasta (page 214)
or
Butternut gnocchi with roasted capsicum sauce & chilli–garlic walnuts (page 156)

Caramelised white chocolate, coconut & passionfruit crème brûlées (page 180)

A few friends to dinner

Baba ganoush with syrupy figs & walnuts (page 74)

Stuffed aubergines with crimson sauce & green caper oil (page 140)
or
Monkfish laksa with Thai basil & curry leaves (page 115)

Fig baklava nests with orange blossom syrup (page 199)

Cooking with the kids

Ultimate vegan burgers (page 164)
or
Drunken meatballs (page 123)

Salted chocolate, hazelnut & muscovado cookies (page 183)

Long lunch with legends

Sweetcorn & kūmara fritters with beetroot borani (page 98)

Herb, onion & hazelnut cheesecake with blistered tomatoes (page 154)

Black sesame, rose & cardamom cake with honey mascarpone icing (page 179)
or
Saffron yoghurt panna cotta with honey-mint oranges & almond crumble (page 186)

Party time

Baked chickpea, leek & potato samosas with toasted coconut & coriander chutney (page 86)
or
Fennel-pepper fried chicken with spicy mandarin sauce (page 167)

Portobello tacos with roasted cherry salsa & avocado cream (page 46)
or
Gochujang beef & shiitake pizza (page 85)

Pistachio, lime & raspberry cake (page 195)

Feeling festive

Chilli, basil & olive overnight focaccia (page 53)

Showstopper cauli with speedy satay & hazelnut dukkah (page 44)

Turmeric roast potatoes with crispy kawakawa & brown butter whip (page 58)

Killer beans with lemongrass, cashews & kaffir lime (page 66)

Harissa roast lamb with minted pomegranate gravy (page 171)
or
Butternut & aubergine snake with basil & pistachio pesto (page 148)

Christmas meringue roulade with rosé cherries & chantilly cream (page 210)
or
Chilli, chocolate & orange 'impossible' cake (page 206)

Big things come in small packages

Many of the recipes in this book pack a bit of extra punch thanks to the smaller things that support the main event. Each of these little flavour rippers are worth making in their own right, to have on standby in your fridge or pantry to amp up a meal from ordinary to extraordinary in an instant.

Oils and condiments

Burger sauce (page 164)

Chilli oil (page 71)

Chilli-lime syrup (page 25)

Green caper oil (page 140)

Green goblin oil (page 96)

Massaman paste (page 124)

Preserved lemon mayo (page 38)

Sour yoghurt (page 150)

Salsas, spreads, whips and dips

Apricot guac (page 31)

Avocado feta whip (page 23)

Basil & pistachio pesto (page 148)

Beetroot borani (page 98)

Brown butter whip (page 58)

Green olive hummus (page 120)

Mango salsa (page 142)

Olive tapenade (page 68)

Roasted cherry salsa (page 46)

Sesame labneh (page 65)

Spring onion cannellini purée (page 50)

Sumac feta whip (page 107)

Triple black hummus (page 107)

Sauces and dressings

Feijoa dressing (page 49)

Grapefruit, mint & ginger dressing (page 92)

Harissa yoghurt dressing (page 57)

Hazelnut romesco (page 81)

Midnight dressing (page 93)

Miso dressing (page 82)

Sesame & miso dressing (page 89)

Sesame-orange sauce (page 79)

Speedy satay (page 44)

Spicy mandarin sauce (page 167)

Tamarind sauce (page 65)

Toasted coconut & coriander chutney (page 86)

Zhug (page 73)

Sprinkles and crunchy things

Cajun seeds (page 116)

Chai spice mix (page 204)

Chilli-garlic walnuts (page 156)

Crispy shallots (page 152)

Crunchy chickpeas (page 96)

Hazelnut dukkah (page 44)

Mint gremolata (page 138)

Pecan pangrattato (page 111)

Sticky cashews (page 79)

Za'atar (page 61)

Sweet release

Almond crumble (page 186)

Balsamic cherries (page 34)

Cardamom ginger ice cream (page 176)

Honey-mint oranges (page 186)

Rosé cherries (page 210)

Rum caramel (page 176)

Spiced mango custard (page 192)

Tahini cream (page 204)

Index

Acknowledgements

It seems a long time ago that I announced on national television I was planning to release a cookbook (what was I thinking?!). While the dream has finally arrived, it's fair to say I was naive to just how much time, energy and resources go into creating a fully realised book like this. (For me, the recipes have always been the easy part, something that comes naturally.) It's the photography, styling, writing, rewriting, editing, and designing, all of which would not have been a success without the incredible team I've had supporting me in creating *Good Vibes*.

It's the photos that make any cookbook shine, and I owe a lot to Aaron McLean for his skills in capturing my food in a fun and contemporary way. To Holly Hunter (commissioning editor extraordinaire!), Alex Hedley, and the entire HarperCollins NZ team for believing in my vision and turning my ideas into something beautiful and accessible. Thank you to George Saad for his design and illustrative talents, particularly the cover that embodies the spirit of the book.

I love Aotearoa, and we have some extraordinary ceramicists in our country whom I wanted to showcase alongside my food. The following people kindly loaned their tableware and pottery for this project, and I want to formally acknowledge their talents and generosity: Ama Adansi-Pipim (Auckland), Bridget at Black Shed Pottery (Waihi), Diane Allen (Auckland), Fiona Mogridge (Auckland), Gabriela Bau-Stubbs (Auckland), Staci Coble (Auckland) and Vanessa Ceelen (Auckland). Thanks also to the team at Cuisine Magazine and The Props Department for your contributions.

To the friends in Whangārei (where I was based when creating *Good Vibes*) who maintained my morale and ate all the leftovers when no one else would, especially: Corey, Mandy and Anna for dogsitting Beau; Holly for sewing all the linen featured; Ben, Ish, Mercy and Rita for being exceptional models; Robbie (+ Issy) for saving the day with oranges, lemons and those two cans of coconut cream.

The biggest thank you of all goes to my day ones who have backed me all the way and continue to inspire me. To Mum, Dad and Oliver, I don't tell you this enough but I love you and feel blessed to call you my family. To my handsome partner Alex, and equally handsome greyhound Beau. You've kept me grounded through the whirlwind this book created. Thank you for your tolerance and unconditional love, and encouraging me to live my dreams.

Lastly, to you, who have persisted right to the bottom of this acknowledgements page. I hope these recipes fill your kitchen with *Good Vibes*, and the deliciousness is shared with friends and whānau for years to come.

ALBY HAILES